UNVENTIONAL

IDEAS TOO GOOD
TO PATENT

FROM THE WORLD'S GREATEST INVENTOR

Tom Giesler

giesler & geisler
berkeley

for Lori, Owen, and Aaron

special thanks to Andy, Nicole, Cristal, Meg, and Paul

www.gieslerandgeisler.com

Cover art by Tom Giesler
Cover design by Amanda Richmond
Interior design by Tom Giesler

ISBN 978-1508834632

Table of Contents

Foreword

Unventional is a "must have" for devotees of satirical humor and precise illustration. It tackles, with wit and invention, the serious problems coming our way as the world's population explodes and its resources implode. (Of course, one hopes that Mr. Giesler hasn't done harm to his tongue as he firmly lodges it in his cheek.)

As a frustrated wannabe inventor myself, and author of *Al Jaffee's Mad Inventions*, I was particularly smitten by the ingenious problem solving imagined in this book. Each remarkable invention is described in easy-to-follow language. The illustrations are exquisite examples of patent application art. They too are easy to follow and understand. The reader's reward is a fascinating look into seemingly practical solutions to universal problems, all depicted in an amusing and entertaining fashion.

Let me cite a typical example.

"Solar glasses—A device worn on or around the face and head that provides sun protection and solar electricity."

The crystal-clear illustrations depict multiple sunglass designs made of solar panels, which capture the sun's energy, convert it into electricity, and power various electronic devices in the wearer's possession.

Other chapters deal with environmental problems that concern us all. In addition to using solar energy in our daily lives, Mr. Giesler also demonstrates harnessing wind power. Water, one of the world's most vital and endangered resources, is ingeniously recycled in everyday activities. Emissions and waste of every variety are reused continuously. What more could an ardent environmentalist ask for?

But you don't have to be an ardent environmentalist, inventor, or professional do-gooder. You just need to have a sharp sense of humor to thoroughly enjoy this fun-filled, well-written, illustrated guide to solving all our problems.

al Jaffee

Award-winning cartoonist, satirist, *MAD Magazine* "Fold-In" creator.

Introduction

The book you are holding is monumental. Critics have hailed it as "unbelievable," "curious," and even "bewildering." Whatever it is, this book offers a paradigm shift so big it can't wait to go through the usual process of vetting, like research, development, clinical trials, etc.

Sometimes an idea is so big that it requires rewriting the playbook. *unventional* is just that big.

In the wake of this book, inventions will no longer be owned, but freely shared. Patents will no longer be filed with the Patent and Trade Office, but cast like seeds into the public wind.

In this book I am offering, free of charge, 40 Remarkable Galaxy-Saving Inventions, all yours for the taking.

No, your eyes are not playing tricks on you—you read that correctly. The inventions in this book are **free**.

And this is an equal-opportunity movement. Garage inventors: run, don't walk, to your workbenches. Hobbyists: warm your glue guns. Multinational corporations: cut funding to lower-priority projects and pump resources into these inventions, and appoint me to your boards of directors. We need all hands on deck.

You might be asking yourself, "Why would a renowned inventor, the envy of his peers and in the midst of a notable career, suddenly begin giving away his inventions for free?"

Well, the story begins before my birth.

Thomas von Giesler
Thomas von Giesler
Inventor

PART ONE
A Visual History

Chapter I
An Introduction to My Family

My name is Thomas von Giesler, and I am
the proud offspring of an inventor who is
the proud offspring of an inventor.

My offspring will all be proud inventors.

Inventor: Thomas Von Giesler
Title: NANO-MATRYOSHKA DOLL SET
Filed: June 9, 2001

REJECTED

GEERTJE VAN DE LAAR TIJN VAN DE LAAR GERDA VAN MORRISON TIEDE VAN MORRISON TINI VAN LEEUWENHOEK

TJEERD
VAN BEETHOVEN

TJAARD
VAN BEETHOVEN

GISELA
VAN JOVI

THEOFILUS
VAN JOVI

THOMAS
VAN ZANDT

TINEKE
VAN ZANDT

GREET
VAN ZANDT

GRIET
VAN HALEN

GODELIEVE
VAN HALEN

GUSTA
VAN HALEN

TEUNIS
VAN DROSS

GERTRUIDA
VAN DROSS

TOBIAS
VAN GEELEN

GEERTA
VAN GEELEN

THOMAS
VON GIESLER

mm 1 2 3 4

FIG. 1

For generations my family has been improving
the quality of life for individuals through our patents.

It all began with Tobias van Geelen, my grandfather.
He was the impressive man who invented
the Waterfowl Cloak for the army in 1932.

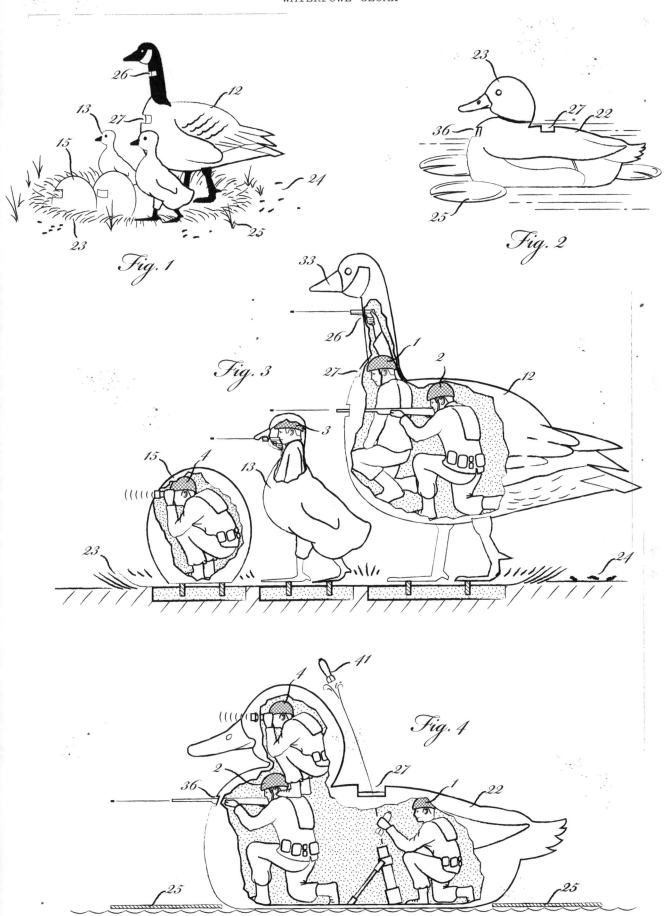

Fig. 1

Fig. 2

Fig. 3

Fig. 4

Grandfather went on to patent several other less-notable inventions
but finally retired a wealthy man after patenting
the Eel Tube in 1956.

Tobias van Geelen
EEL TUBE

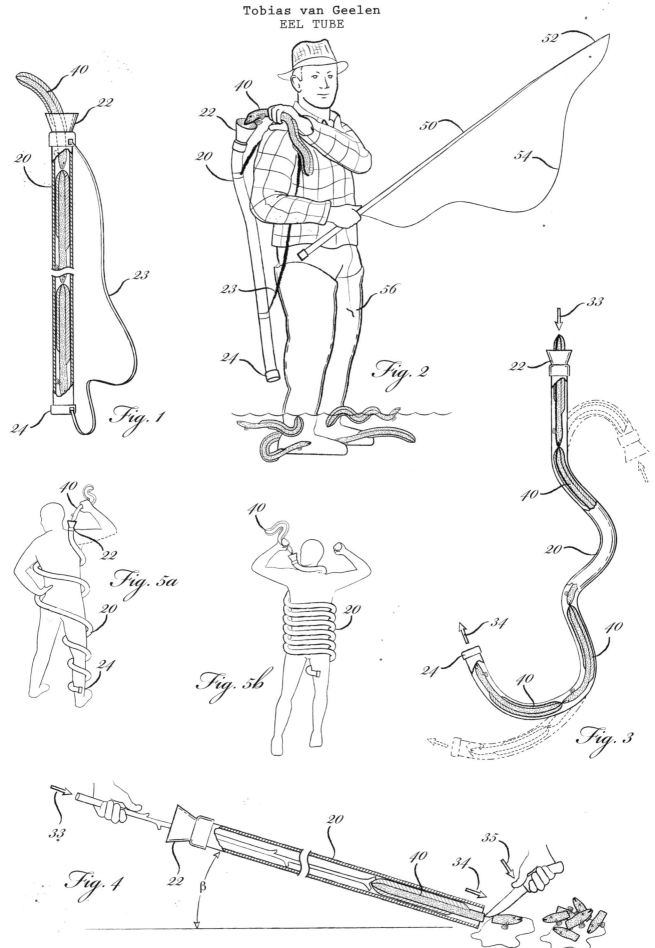

Fig. 1

Fig. 2

Fig. 3

Fig. 4

Fig. 5a

Fig. 5b

My mother, Geerta van Geelen, was a fastidious
and very practical woman. She bolstered my family's reputation
with her patented "Clothing's Clothing" in 1965.

G. van Geelen
Clothing's Clothing

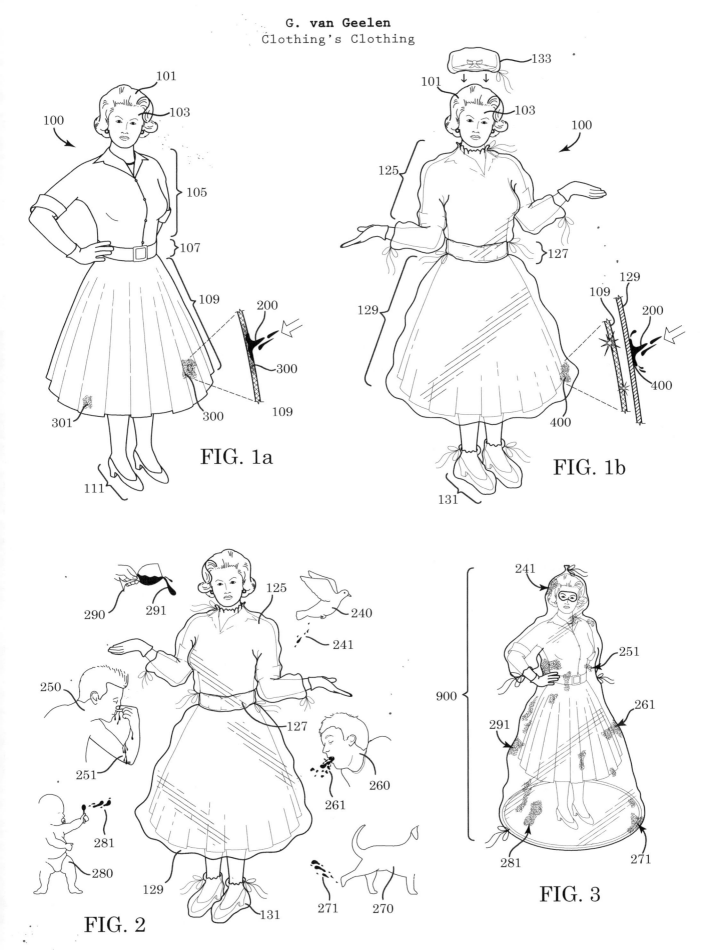

FIG. 1a

FIG. 1b

FIG. 2

FIG. 3

In 1967, Mother married Father, Theobald von Giesler,
a heavily bearded gentleman.

That same year she invented the Mustache Manager.

G. von Giesler
Mustache Manager

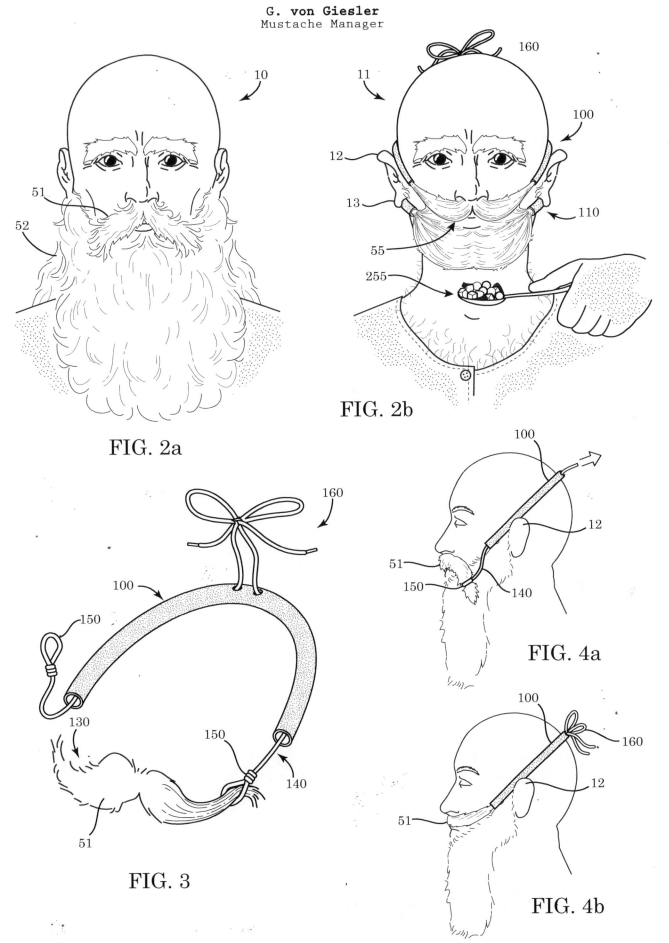

FIG. 2a

FIG. 2b

FIG. 3

FIG. 4a

FIG. 4b

Later that year, Mother invented Serving Skins.

This revolutionary patent was likely the inspiration for future breakthroughs, such as disposable shower caps, Ziploc sandwich bags, and sanitary toilet-seat covers.

G. von Giesler
Serving skins

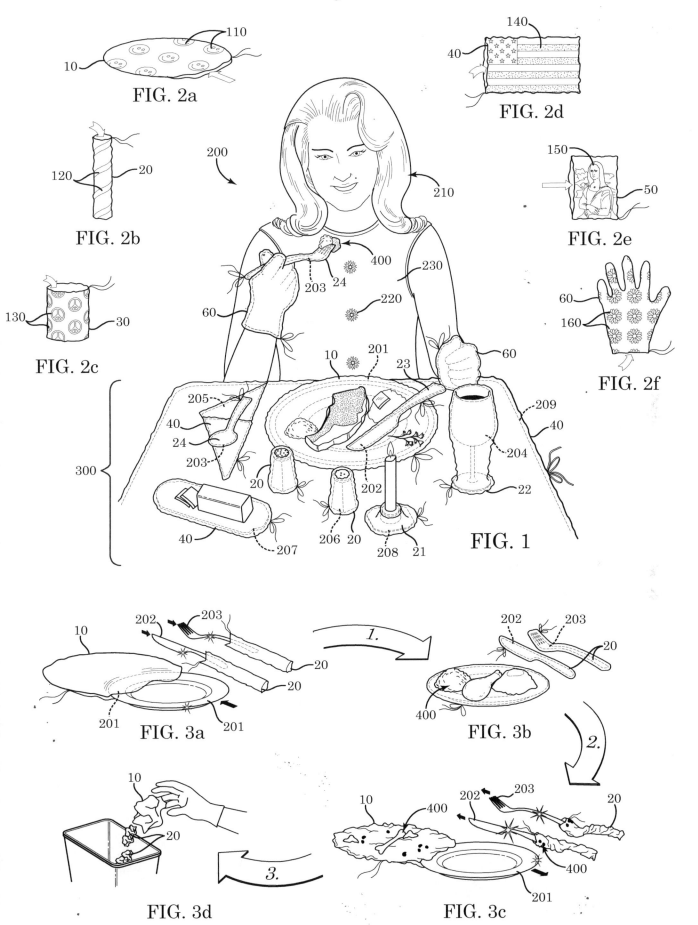

FIG. 2a

FIG. 2b

FIG. 2c

FIG. 2d

FIG. 2e

FIG. 2f

FIG. 1

FIG. 3a

FIG. 3b

FIG. 3c

FIG. 3d

In 1968, the year I was born, Mother invented Baby Wrap. Many believe this invention laid the groundwork for modern disposable diapers.

And so it seemed destined from the moment of my birth that I, too, would one day invent great things.

G. von Giesler
Baby Wrap

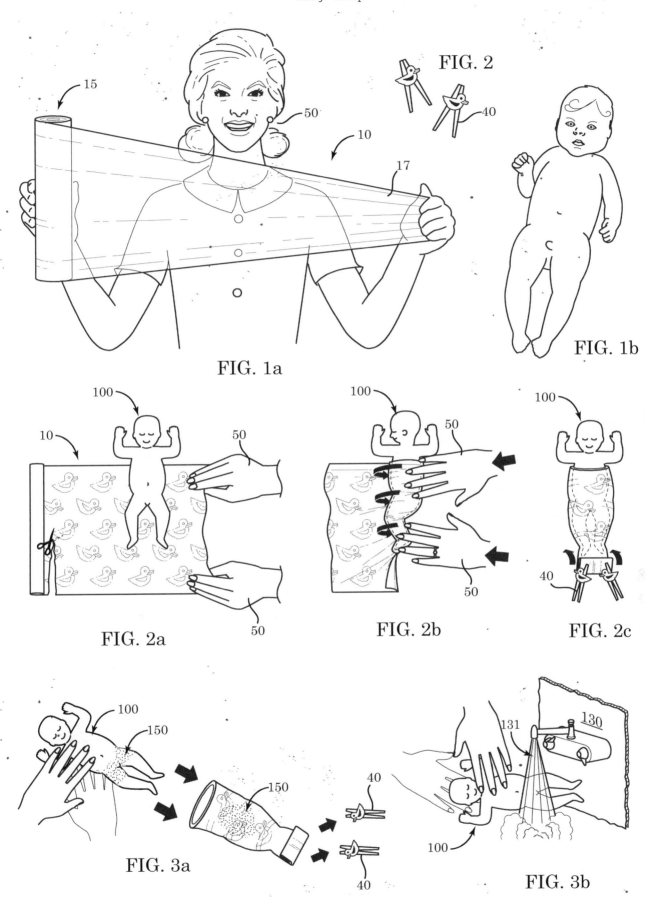

FIG. 2

FIG. 1a

FIG. 1b

FIG. 2a

FIG. 2b

FIG. 2c

FIG. 3a

FIG. 3b

Chapter II.
An Introduction to Myself

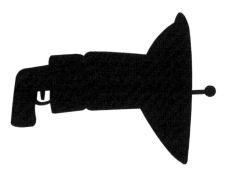

I was a very inquisitive child, spending all of my free time
experimenting in the family laboratory.

Even before I could write a patent myself, I had already invented
the Baby Brother Vanishing Ray at the age of 6...

...and Sugar Vegetables at the age of 9.

Sugar Vegetables

In 1983, while attending junior high school, my idea for the Concentration Book came to me in science class. The invention was a huge hit with my classmates, so I immediately filed for my first patent.

Though this idea was denied, I continued to try to patent my inventions through the 1980s and '90s.

To: U.S. Patent Office

Thomas D. W. von Giesler
Title: Concentration Book
Date: April 26, 1983

REJECTED

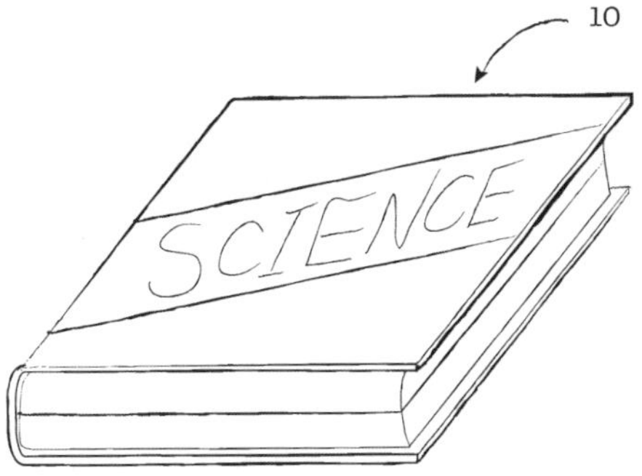
10
SCIENCE

Figure 1a

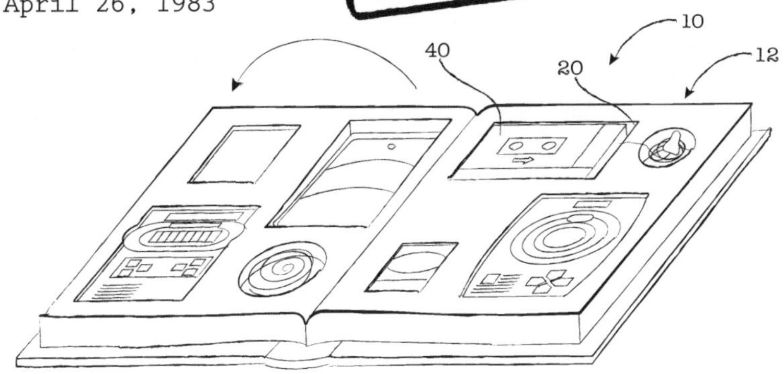
10
40
20
12

Figure 1b

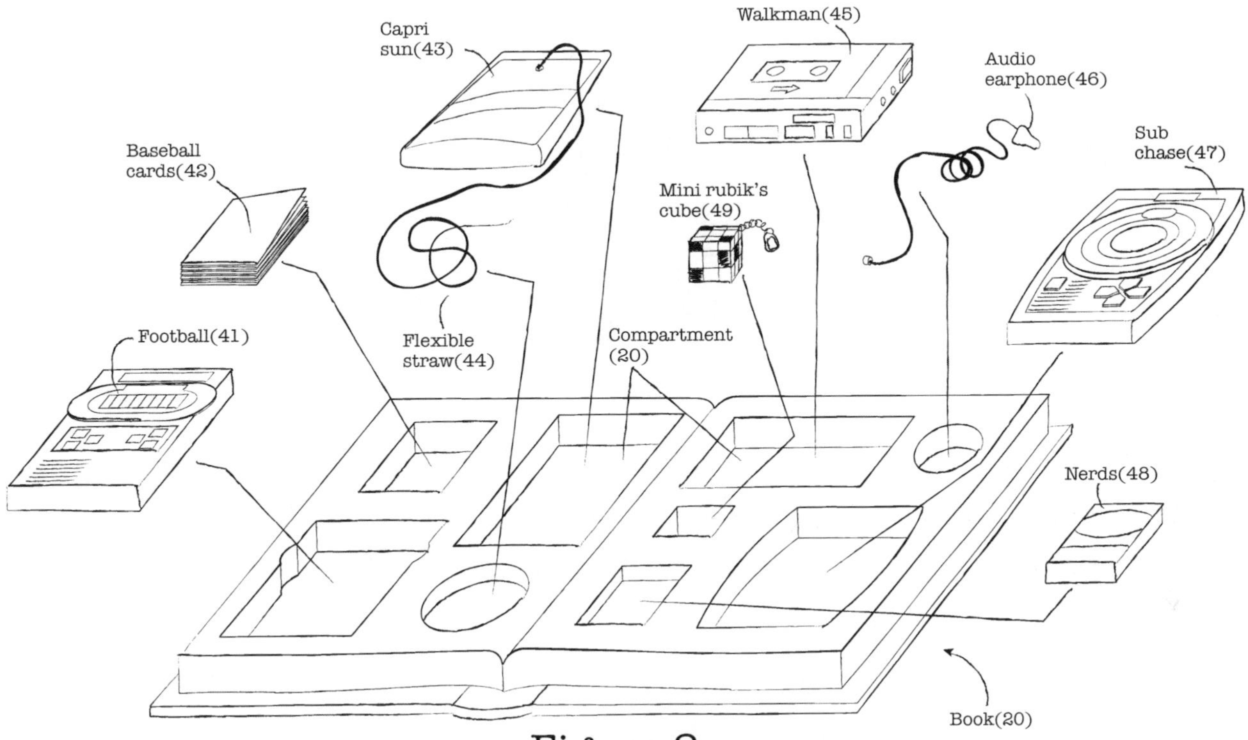
Capri sun(43)
Walkman(45)
Audio earphone(46)
Baseball cards(42)
Sub chase(47)
Mini rubik's cube(49)
Football(41)
Flexible straw(44)
Compartment (20)
Nerds(48)
Book(20)

Figure 2

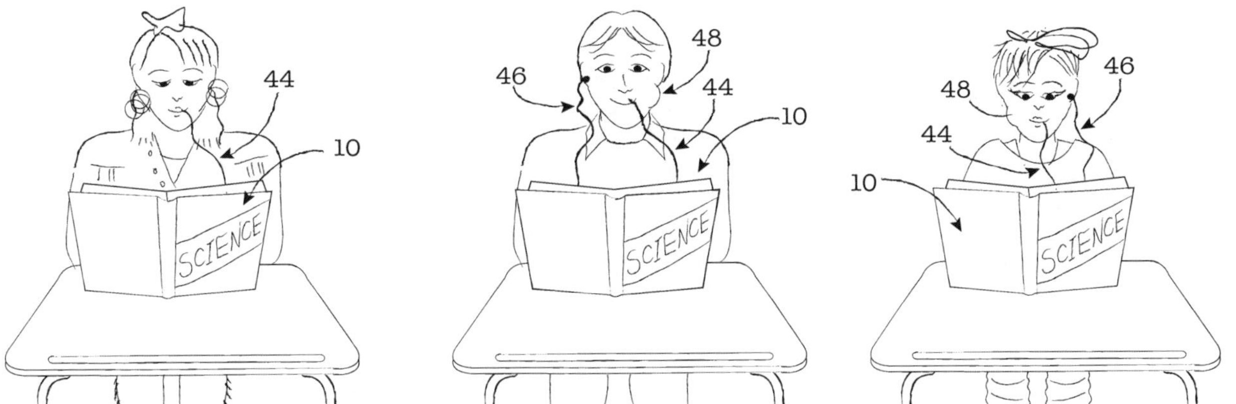
44
10
SCIENCE
48
46
44
10
SCIENCE
46
48
44
10
SCIENCE

Figure 3

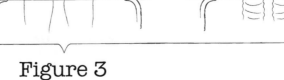

The late 1990s brought me great inspiration and moved me
ever closer to realizing my first patent and founding a start-up.
The Semi-Mobile Information Superhighway Phone invention,
a handheld device that combined email,
web, and telephonic connectivity, was a pioneering innovation.

A lack of sufficient public electrical outlets was the unforeseen
obstacle that ultimately killed the idea.

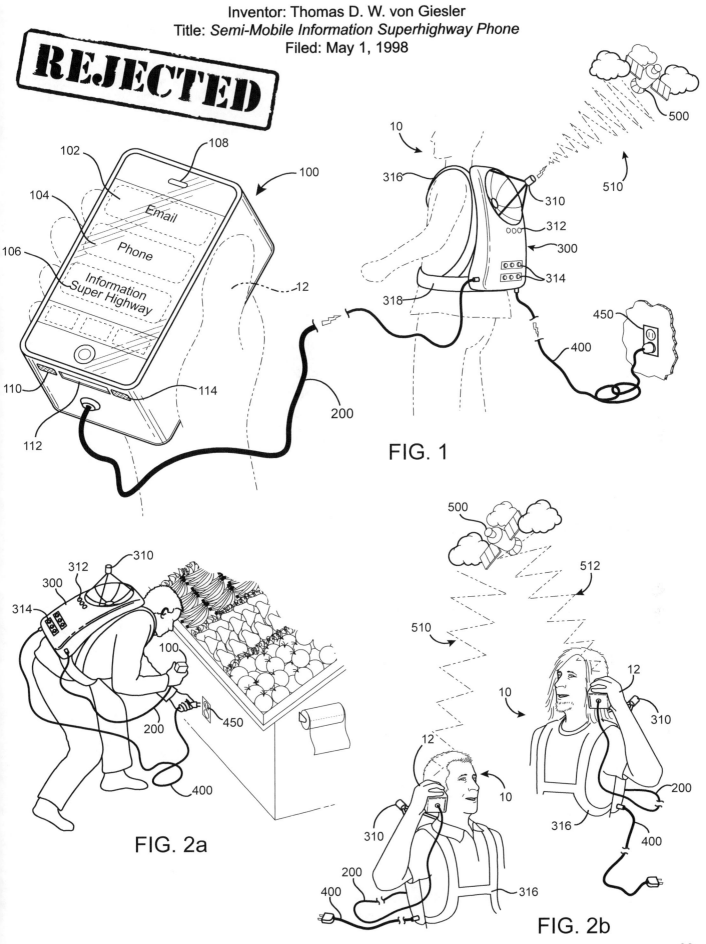

REJECTED

FIG. 1

FIG. 2a

FIG. 2b

Email

Phone

Information
Super Highway

My Semi-Mobile Information Superhighway Watch
encountered similar setbacks.

Inventor: Thomas D. W. von Giesler
Title: *Semi-Mobile Information Superhighway Watch*
Filed: May 2, 1998

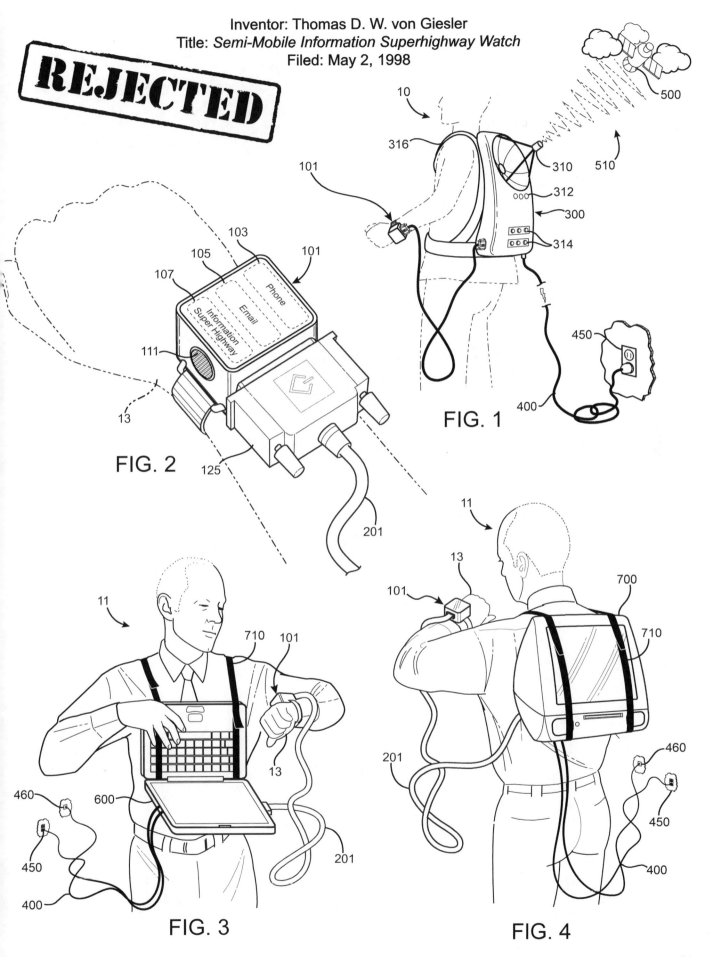

REJECTED

FIG. 1

FIG. 2

FIG. 3

FIG. 4

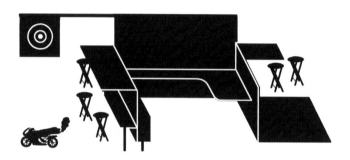

Next, I turned my attention to improving corporate working conditions with Party Cubicle and marketed the idea to several prominent corporations around the United States.

Inventor: Thomas D. W. von Giesler
Title: *Party Cubicle*
Filed: Feb. 8, 1999

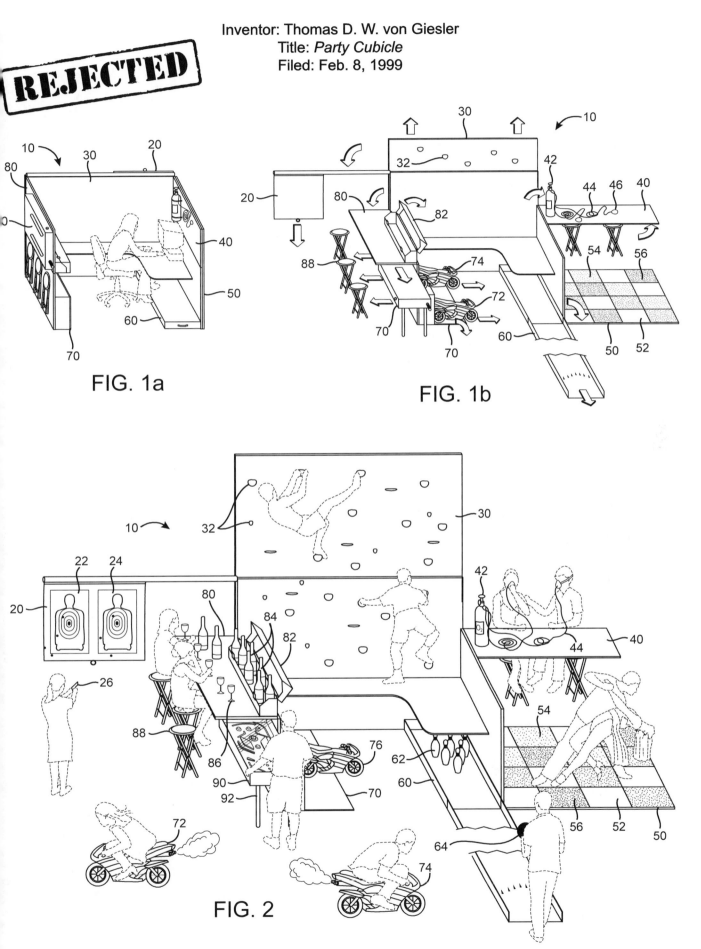

FIG. 1a

FIG. 1b

FIG. 2

Then, in the year 2000, I finally hit it big with my first actual patent. The 3D Comb for Hair was manufactured and briefly given away as a promotion by a popular online pet-supply store.

This was just the springboard I needed to get higher visibility for my ideas so that I could start making a difference in people's lives.

United States Patent

von Giesler

3D Comb for Hair

US00D4211703

Patent Number: Des. 421,1703
Date of Patent: Jan. 23, 2000

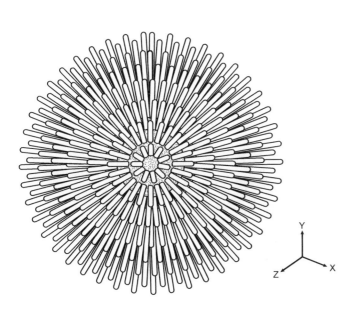

FIG. 1

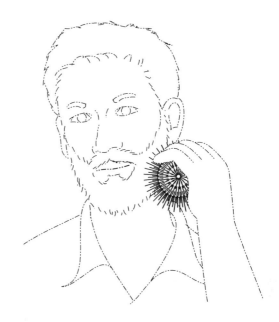

FIG. 2

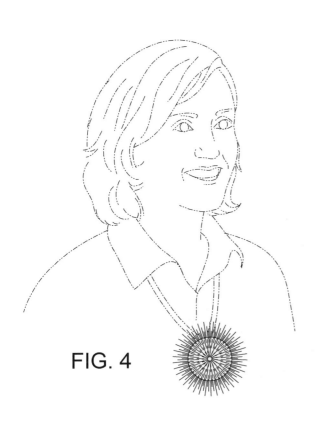

FIG. 4

FIG. 3

35

In 2003 I collaborated with a Brazilian firm on my brainchild. My "See No. Hair No. Smell No." device, a clean-burning butane ear-hair removal system, was a cosmetological breakthrough.

My future looked bright.

United States Patent

von Giesler

Clean-Burning Ear-Hair Removal Device

US6,666,8569

Patent Number: US 6,666,8569

Date of Patent: Oct. 06, 2003

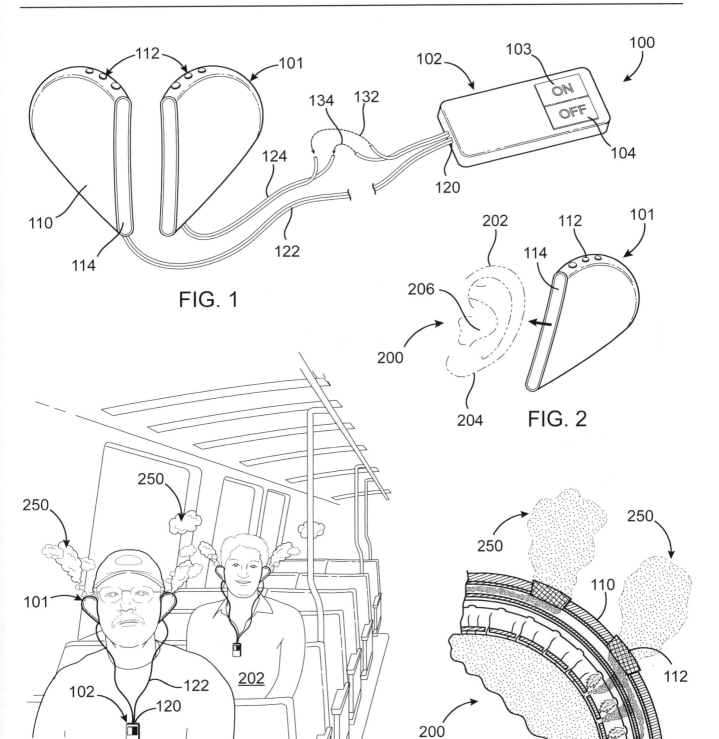

FIG. 1

FIG. 2

FIG. 3

FIG. 4

Quite unexpectedly, however, I spent the next three years fighting lawsuits filed by unsatisfied customers. I maintained my innocence throughout the proceedings, insisting that the device was clearly designed and marketed for ear use only.

Although I was finally acquitted in 2006, the episode led me to rethink my method of helping people.

At that moment it became apparent to me that the centuries-old model of intellectual proprietorship was broken. My inventions clearly had the power to improve lives, but frivolous lawsuits could continue to prevent them from doing so.

Lending a helping hand to my fellow man had never seemed so perilous.

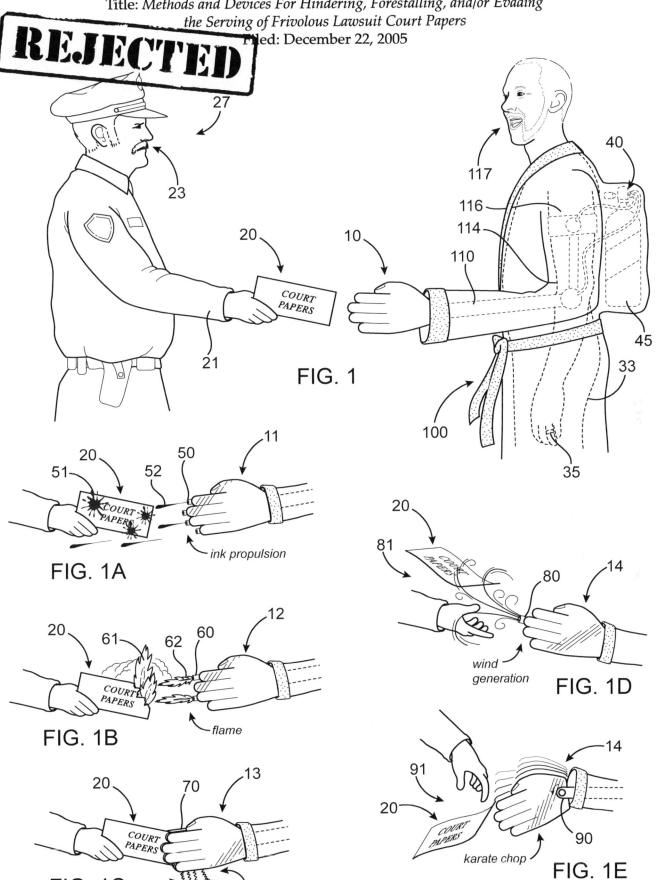

REJECTED

FIG. 1

FIG. 1A
ink propulsion

FIG. 1B
flame

FIG. 1C
document shredder

FIG. 1D
wind generation

FIG. 1E
karate chop

Then, in a sudden burst of clarity, I realized I had lost sight of
the proverbial "forest" for all of its litigious "trees." I wasn't put on
this planet to save people; I was put on this planet to save planets.
(Besides, planets don't sue people—people sue people.)

My mission became crystal clear: fix the forest, not the trees.
And all I would need is a global team to bring
this ambitious enterprise to fruition.

REJECTED

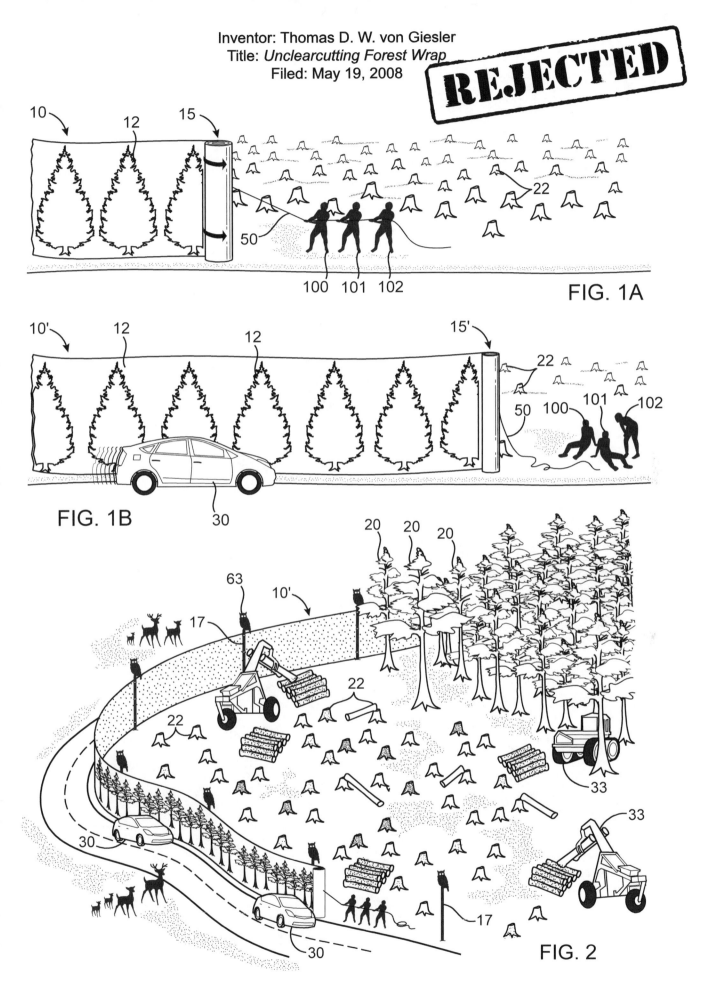

FIG. 1A

FIG. 1B

FIG. 2

But what incentive could I offer to enlist the brightest, most energetic and entrepreneurial citizens of our planet to do the legwork for my new venture?

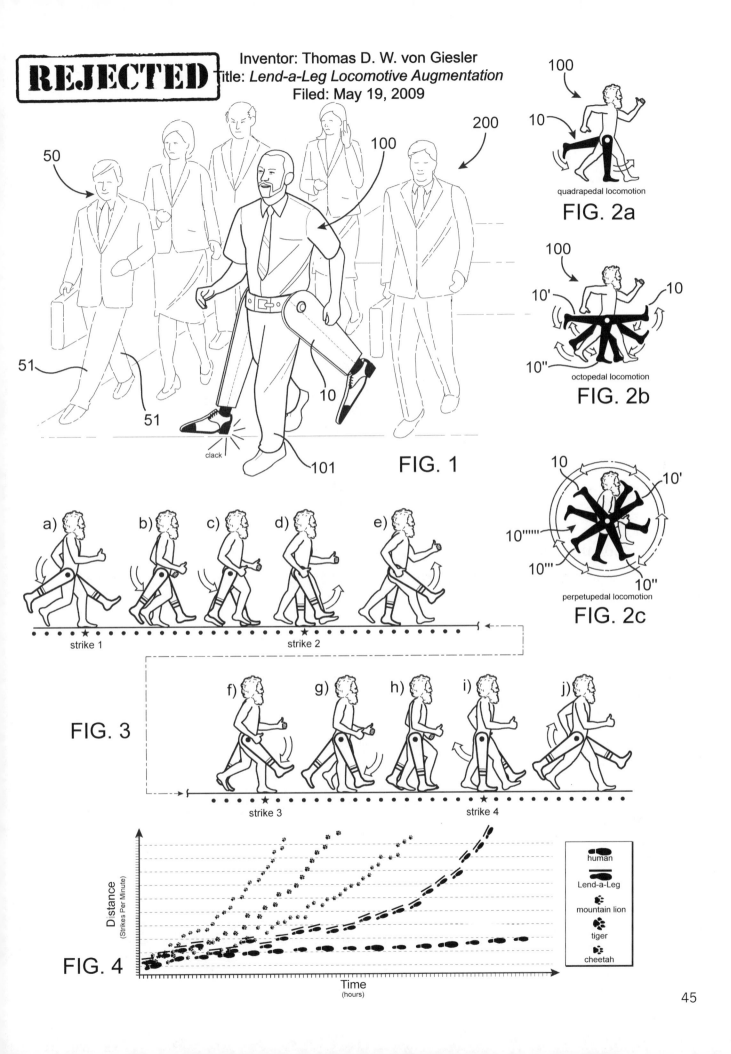

REJECTED

Inventor: Thomas D. W. von Giesler
Title: *Lend-a-Leg Locomotive Augmentation*
Filed: May 19, 2009

FIG. 1

clack

FIG. 2a
quadrapedal locomotion

FIG. 2b
octopedal locomotion

FIG. 2c
perpetupedal locomotion

FIG. 3

a) b) c) d) e)

strike 1   strike 2

f) g) h) i) j)

strike 3   strike 4

FIG. 4

Distance
(Strikes Per Minute)

Time
(hours)

human
Lend-a-Leg
mountain lion
tiger
cheetah

45

Well, what if I offered the greatest gift my family could ever bestow upon humanity: my ideas...for free.

It's true. Now every earth-loving being on our planet will have the seeds to start the green company of his or her dreams— free of charge.

Inventor: Thomas D. W. von Giesler
Title: *Method for Soil-less, Water-less, Effortless Aeroponic Agriculture*
Filed: December 25, 2010

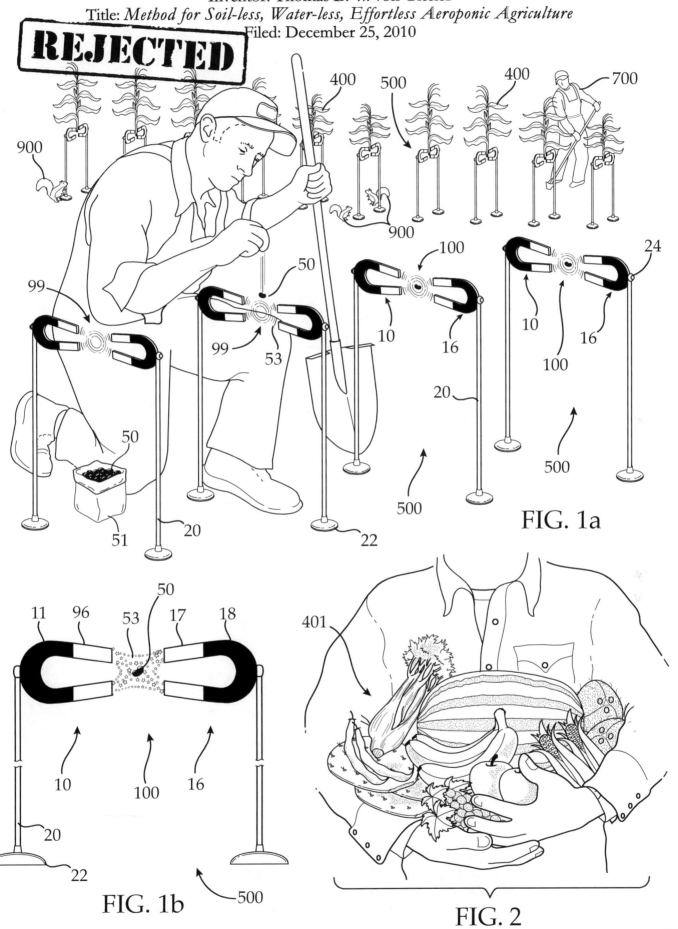

FIG. 1a

FIG. 1b

FIG. 2

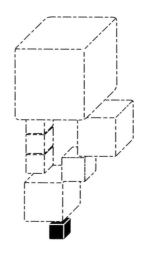

I'm not kidding.

The unique inventions in the following chapters are yours to take
and build upon, à la opensource and freeware.
Each of my free inventions offers a solid blueprint for a sustainable
future on earth and beyond, leaving just a few minor details to be
sorted out through your R&D.

Finally, I can sit back, free of any liability whatsoever,
and watch as my unique vision reshapes the planet.

Inventor: Thomas D. W. von Giesler
Title: *Building Block*
Filed: March 01, 2011

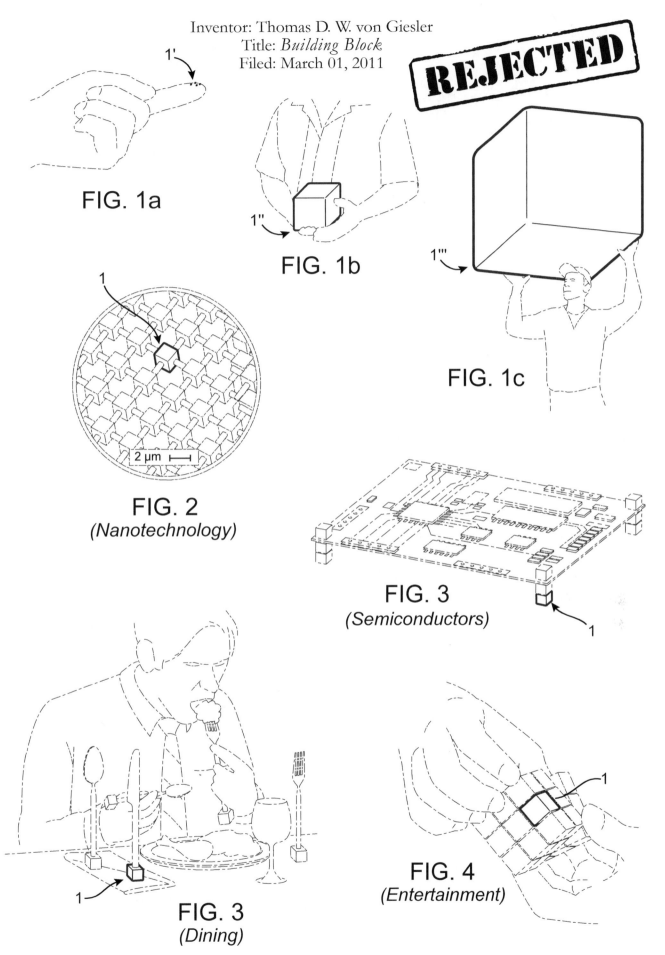

FIG. 1a

FIG. 1b

REJECTED

FIG. 1c

FIG. 2
(Nanotechnology)

FIG. 3
(Semiconductors)

FIG. 3
(Dining)

FIG. 4
(Entertainment)

Inventor: Thomas D. W. von Giesler
Title: *Building Block*
Filed: March 01, 2011

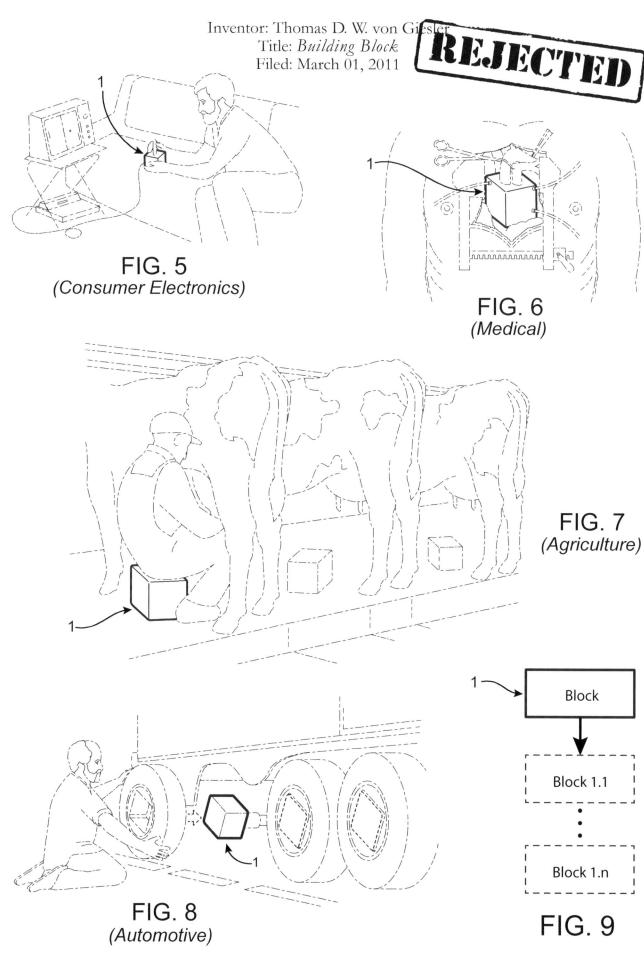

FIG. 5
(Consumer Electronics)

FIG. 6
(Medical)

FIG. 7
(Agriculture)

FIG. 8
(Automotive)

FIG. 9

Inventor: Thomas D. W. von Giesler
Title: *Building Block*
Filed: March 01, 2011

REJECTED

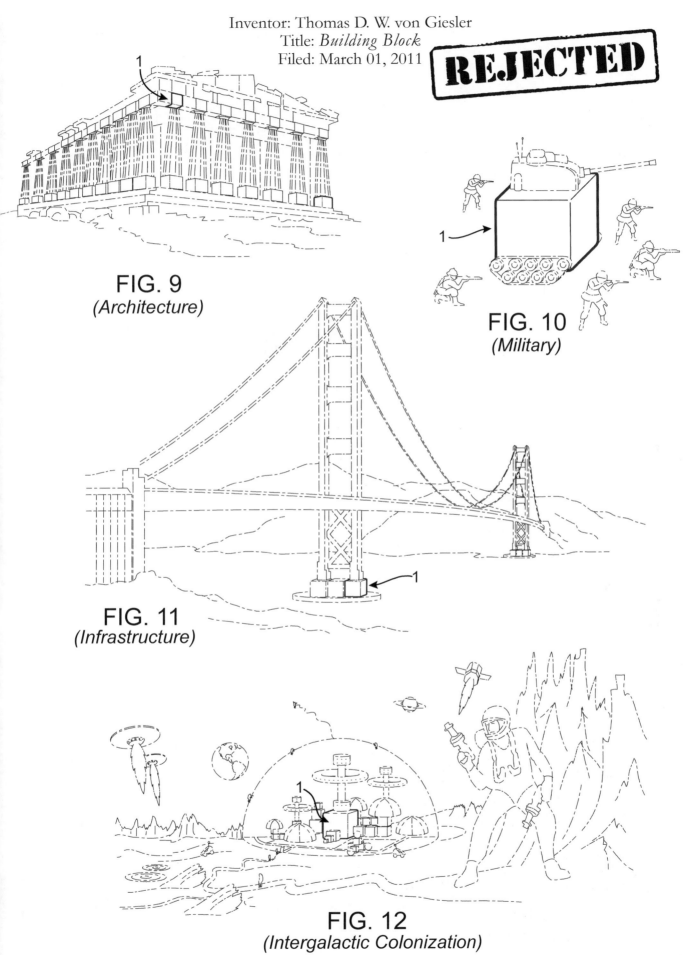

FIG. 9
(Architecture)

FIG. 10
(Military)

FIG. 11
(Infrastructure)

FIG. 12
(Intergalactic Colonization)

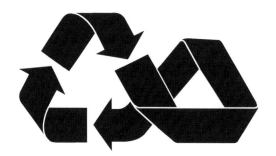

So, it has come to pass. A new tomorrow begins today.

We have important work to do here,
so we should get started right away.

I'm excited to be working with you.

I hope you are excited, too.

unventionally yours,

Thomas Von Giesler

Total & Utter Liability Release Form

1. I HEREBY WAIVE AND RELEASE ANY AND ALL CLAIMS that I or my heirs have or may have in the future against Thomas D. W. von Giesler for any loss, damage, expense, or injury, including death, suffered from or in connection to the implementation or use of the inventions herein due to any cause whatsoever, INCLUDING NEGLIGENCE ON THE PART OF Mr. von Giesler;_____ (initials) 2. I HEREBY RELIEVE Mr. von Giesler FROM ANY DUTY TO PROTECT ME FROM HARM, and agree that even if Mr. von Giesler chooses to give instructions for proper use or advice on the safety procedures of the inventions herein, such actions shall not alter the fact that Mr. von Giesler has no duty to protect me._____ (initials) 3. I WILL HOLD HARMLESS AND INDEMNIFY Mr. von Giesler for liability for property damage or personal injury, including death, disfigurement, paralysis, blindness, hair loss, severe allergic reactions (rash; hives; itching; difficulty breathing; tightness in the chest; swelling of the mouth, face, lips, or tongue); chest pain; fainting; fast or irregular heartbeat; memory loss; painful or prolonged erection; ringing in the ears; seizure; severe or persistent dizziness; severe or persistent vision changes; sudden decrease or loss of vision in one or both eyes; sudden hearing loss; constipation; headache; body pain; swelling; corns; ingrown hairs; pimples; anal seepage; vertigo; halitosis; difficulty urinating; flatulence; anxiety; intestinal necrosis; blood in the stool; cardiac arrest, hypotension, tachycardia, palpitations, pulmonary hypertension, pulmonary embolism, vasodilation, vasovagal reaction, cerebrovascular accident, and syncope; neurogenic bladder, hematuria, proteinuria, impotence, depression, sadness, gloominess, fatigue, hangnails, persistent itching, or uncontrollable laughter to myself and any other person resulting from or arising in connection with my use of the inventions herein or equipment produced as a result the patenting of the ideas herein, or participation in activities utilizing hardware produced as a result of the patenting of the ideas herein. _____ (initials) 4. I HAVE READ AND UNDERSTAND the foregoing Inventions Herein Acknowledgment of Risks and have discussed it with my spouse, lover, drinking buddies, barista, parent(s), or guardian(s) and am voluntarily signing below. If I am signing on behalf of a comrade, I represent and warrant that I am doing so with the consent and approval of my spouse (if any), and I understand that I am acknowledging the risks to my comrade. I have read and understand this Agreement and intend that it be binding on me and my heirs, executors, administrators, familial acquaintances, and assigns. By signing this Agreement, I intend to waive legal rights against Mr. von Giesler on behalf of myself and my heirs, executors, administrators, cohorts, and assigns. PARENTS OR GUARDIANS OF CONSUMERS UNDER AGE 18 MUST SIGN THIS SECTION AND INITIAL ALL BLANKS ON THIS PAGE. I am the parent or guardian of the minor named above. I hereby make and enter into each and every representation, waiver, release, and indemnity described above on behalf of myself, the minor, and any other parent or guardian of the minor. I intend to give up my right, the minor's right, and the right of any other parent or guardian to maintain any claim or suit against Mr. von Giesler arising out of the minor's use of Mr. von Giesler's facilities or equipment, or participation in activities sponsored by Mr. von Giesler. I believe and represent that I HAVE LEGAL AUTHORITY TO MAKE THESE WAIVERS AND RELEASES, and I agree to indemnify Mr. von Giesler for all liability arising out of any lack of authority on my part to make such waivers and releases. Signed this date _____/ _____/ _____.

And if I am a minor, my parent(s), for and on behalf of myself and my children, heirs, executors, administrators, and representatives, agree to release, indemnify and defend Mr. von Giesler with respect to all claims, liabilities, losses, suits, or expenses (including costs and reasonable attorney's fees) made or brought by anyone, including a co-participant, third party, my child, or any members of my or my child's family arising out of any injury, damage, death, loss of teeth, or other loss in any way connected with the use or abuse of the inventions herein. This agreement includes any losses claimed to be caused, in whole or in part, by the negligence of Mr. von Giesler. I agree here to waive all claims against Mr. von Giesler, and agree that neither I, nor anyone acting on my behalf, will make a claim or file a lawsuit of any kind against Mr. von Giesler, as a result of any injury, damage, death, or other permanent loss suffered by me or anyone else. I agree to this and all other aspects of my relationship with Mr. von Giesler or this book. Further, any mediation, suit, or other proceeding arising out of or relating to my participation in Mr. von Giesler activities, must be filed exclusively in the State of Ohio, and Ohio State law shall apply. I agree to settle any dispute (that cannot be settled by discussion) through mediation before a mutually acceptable Ohio mediator. I also agree that if I, my associate, or someone on the associate's behalf, assert(s) a claim or file(s) a suit against Mr. von Giesler, I will pay all costs and attorney's fees incurred by Mr. von Giesler in defending that claim or suit, if the claim or suit is withdrawn or dismissed, or to the extent a court determines that Mr. von Giesler is not responsible for the injury or loss. Any portion of this Document deemed unlawful or unenforceable shall not affect the remaining provisions of the Document, and those remaining provisions shall continue in full force and effect. I have carefully read, understand, and voluntarily sign this Document and acknowledge that it shall be effective and binding upon myself and my family, heirs, executors, representatives, and estate. Participant Signature _____ Date _____ Print name here_____ Parent(s) or Guardian(s) must sign below for any participating minor (those under 18 years of age) and agree that they are subject to all the terms of this Document, as set forth above. If I have a participating associate, I understand that my signature here includes my agreement per the terms of this Document to release any claims I may have against Mr. von Giesler, as a result of any injury, damage, death, or other loss suffered by my associate, and to defend and indemnify Mr. von Giesler should my associate, someone on the associate's behalf, or a co-participant or third party, bring a claim against Mr. von Giesler, in any way connected with my associate's participation in Mr. von Giesler's inventions. _____Date_____Print name here _____Date_____Print name here _____

Beware!

You can get hurt using these ideas. If you do not wish to accept the risk of injury or death, then you may return this release unsigned and slowly step away from this book. If you have a medical condition that may affect your ability to safely participate in the reading of this book, please consult your physician before engaging in this activity.

So help you god…

PART TWO

Free Inventions

Chapter III.
Waste and Consumption

Grandmother van Geelen was fond of reciting the proverb
"Waste not, want not." Today, in a time of such great abundance,
we have lost touch with this principle.

Here are some ways we can all start "waste not"-ing.

Burger Sheath

ABSTRACT

A relatively thin, edible membrane of gelatin used as a substitute for fast-food disposable packaging and wrappers.

BACKGROUND OF INVENTION

When was the last time you recycled the burger wrapper from your favorite fast-food restaurant? Most likely, it was never. Fast-food packaging is the least commonly recycled paper product in the world. While most packaging ends up in trash cans, the average American car holds 8.5 square feet of fast-food packaging under seats and between seat cushions. Experts have calculated that if the fast-food wrappers were removed from every U.S. automobile today, we would need to build dozens of new landfills just to accommodate the overflow. It is conceivable that within 15 years, the volume of discarded fast-food packaging in America will surpass the total volume of human beings in America.

The current invention takes discarded wrapping material out of our landfills and puts it where it belongs—in our bellies. Edible gelatin film, applied with aerosol or brush, encases and protects fast-food items. The sheathing material also protects the diner's apparel from accidental splattering of condiments and grease during consumption, thereby eliminating the need for paper napkins. The gelatin can be flavor balanced to enhance the dining experience or colorfully tinted to offer exciting presentation options.

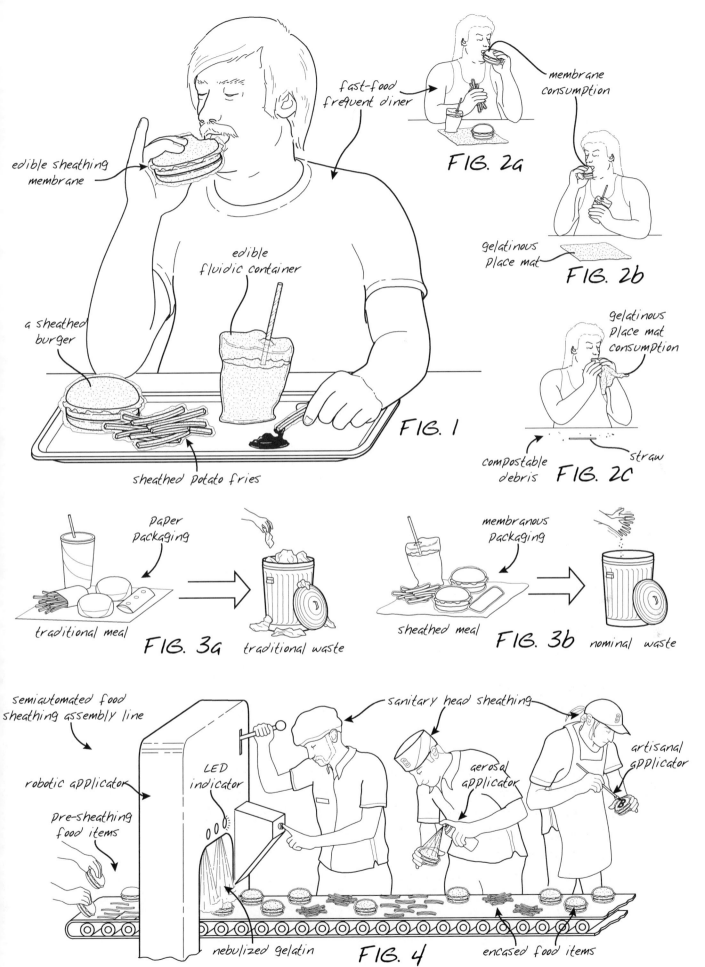

edible sheathing membrane

fast-food frequent diner

membrane consumption

FIG. 2a

gelatinous place mat

FIG. 2b

edible fluidic container

a sheathed burger

sheathed potato fries

FIG. 1

gelatinous place mat consumption

compostable debris

straw

FIG. 2c

paper packaging

traditional meal

FIG. 3a traditional waste

membranous packaging

sheathed meal

FIG. 3b nominal waste

semiautomated food sheathing assembly line

sanitary head sheathing

robotic applicator

LED indicator

aerosol applicator

artisanal applicator

pre-sheathing food items

nebulized gelatin

FIG. 4

encased food items

59

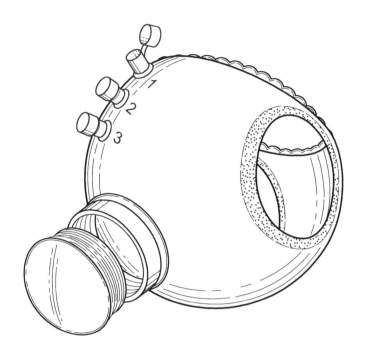

Diaper Bowl

ABSTRACT

A rigid plastic diaper with plumbing cleanout. A host of optional hose fittings can be used for cleansing and disinfecting the interior of the bowl and exterior of the derriere.

BACKGROUND OF INVENTION

Imagine an Olympic-sized swimming pool filled with baby excreta. And imagine a disposable diaper big enough to sop up all of that waste. Now imagine this colossal soiled diaper being dumped into one of our precious landfills. Are you beginning to picture the crisis at the overflowing landfills in the United States? While cloth diapers would protect our landfills from the trillions of diapers discarded every year, laundering them would waste quadrillions of gallons of otherwise clean, drinkable water.

Utilizing resilient materials, the present invention offers an easily maintained, comfortable, extended-use diaper bowl. Attractive enough on its own, the bowl can also be seamlessly integrated into fashionable baby and geriatric clothing.

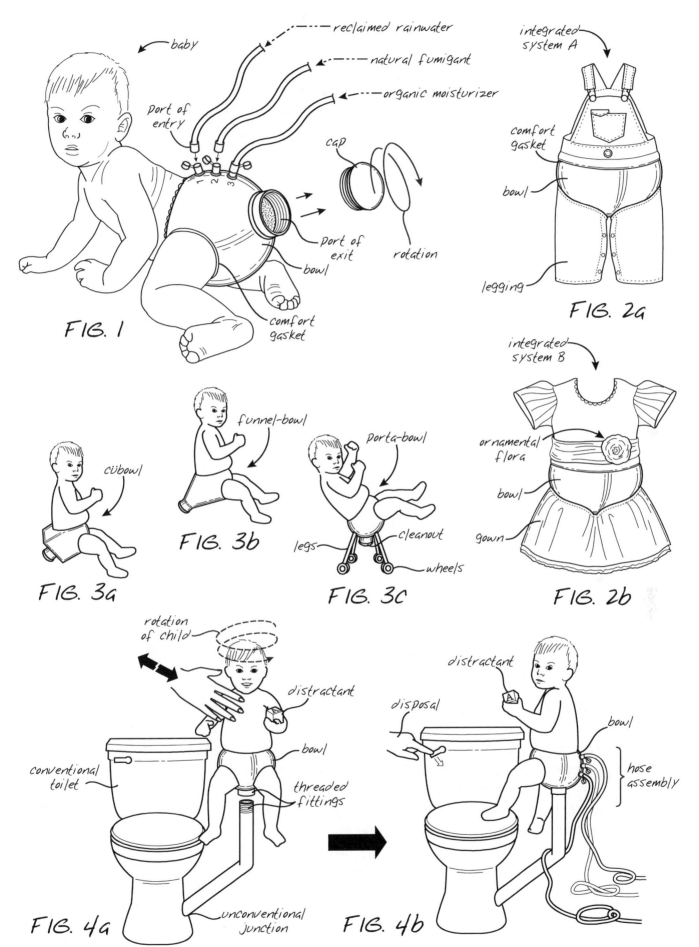

FIG. 1

baby

reclaimed rainwater

natural fumigant

organic moisturizer

Port of entry

cap

rotation

Port of exit

bowl

comfort gasket

FIG. 2a

integrated system A

comfort gasket

bowl

legging

FIG. 3a

cubowl

FIG. 3b

funnel-bowl

FIG. 3c

Porta-bowl

legs

cleanout

wheels

FIG. 2b

integrated system B

ornamental flora

bowl

gown

FIG. 4a

rotation of child

distractant

conventional toilet

bowl

threaded fittings

unconventional junction

FIG. 4b

distractant

disposal

bowl

hose assembly

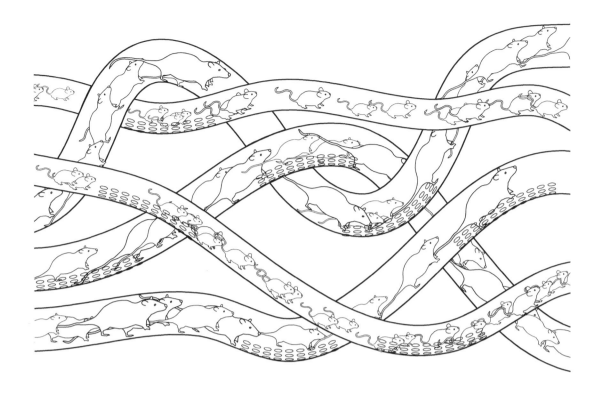

Varmintube

ABSTRACT

A length of flexible tubing with perforations large enough to allow hungry woodland creatures to access and consume compostable materials in one's home. The perforations would ideally be small enough to prevent the animals from exiting the perforations en masse.

BACKGROUND OF INVENTION

Since the advent of garbage disposals in the 1970s, our nation's water treatment plants have been under siege by residential gray water from kitchen sinks. Enormous quantities of residual debris are collected in filtration systems and must be disposed of in one of two ways: incineration, which releases billowing clouds of noxious gas into our skies, or local waterway dumping, which kills everything in its path. The gray water problem could be fixed through residential composting if people were less averse to the smell of rotting compost near their homes.

Taking advantage of an animal's natural instincts to follow a path to food, the current invention utilizes tubing of varying diameters to safely usher wild animals into one's home for compost removal. After satiation, the creatures return to the wild through the same tube to locations a safe distance away, thereby preventing unwanted nesting and colonization in and around the home.

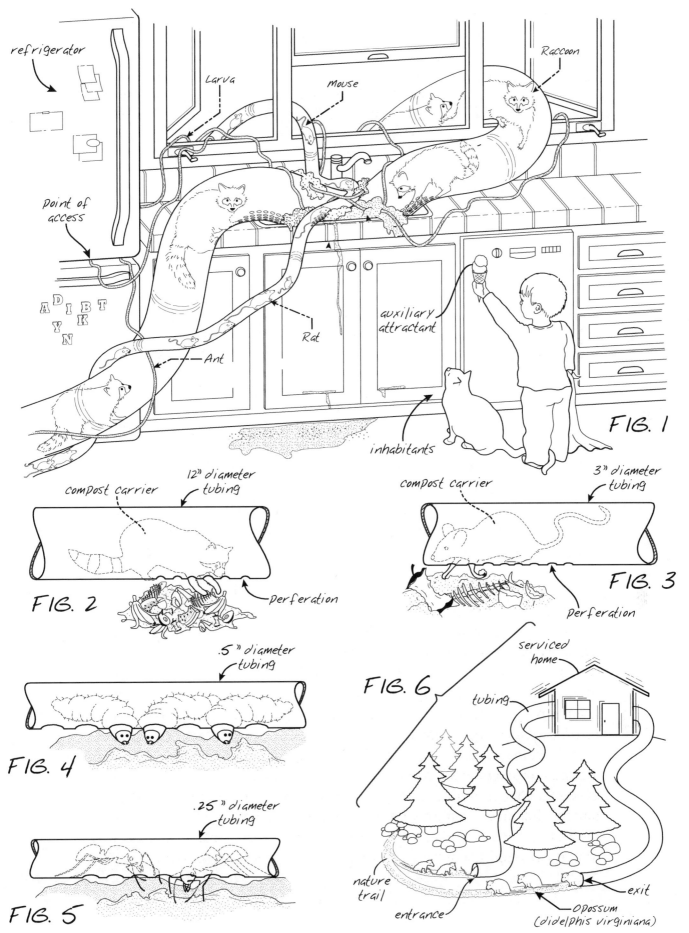

refrigerator

Larva

Mouse

Raccoon

Point of access

A D I B T
Y N
D I K

auxiliary attractant

Rat

Ant

inhabitants

FIG. 1

compost carrier

12" diameter tubing

Perferation

FIG. 2

compost carrier

3" diameter tubing

Perferation

FIG. 3

.5" diameter tubing

FIG. 4

.25" diameter tubing

FIG. 5

FIG. 6

serviced home

tubing

nature trail

entrance

exit

Opossum (didelphis virginiana)

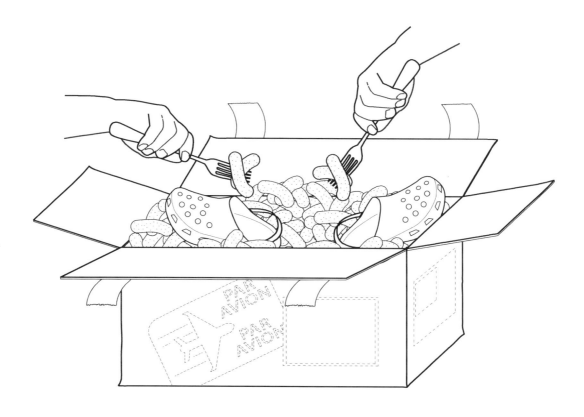

StyroFood

ABSTRACT
Delicious corn-based foam packing material.

BACKGROUND OF INVENTION

Question: What is the difference between *corn puff snacks* and *corn-based packing peanuts*? Answer: One is eaten and one is not—until now.

We all breathed a sigh of relief in the late '90s, when corn-based packing material began arriving in boxes with our online orders. Finally, we thought, an end to the trillions of foam packing peanuts discarded each year. But without a convenient place to compost, we continue to choke our landfills with garbage bags full of biodegradable packing nuts. What we need is a way to keep these packing peanuts in our homes and out of the trash. The current invention offers a delicious solution to this problem. By simply infusing the corn-based packing material with flavor essence, we can make traditional, bland packing peanuts burst with flavor—and nearly irresistible. Just imagine the renewed excitement every time your mail carrier arrives at your door with a box of shoes or books, or an online auction order, packed in free snacks! Finally, consumers can truly *consume* everything in the box. Additionally, foam-peanut factories can modify their machinery to create an endless variety of familiar shapes, like "goldfish crackers" for an after-school snack and "tortilla chips" for your next fiesta. Leftover packing material can simply be ground up and reconstituted for polenta-like dishes.

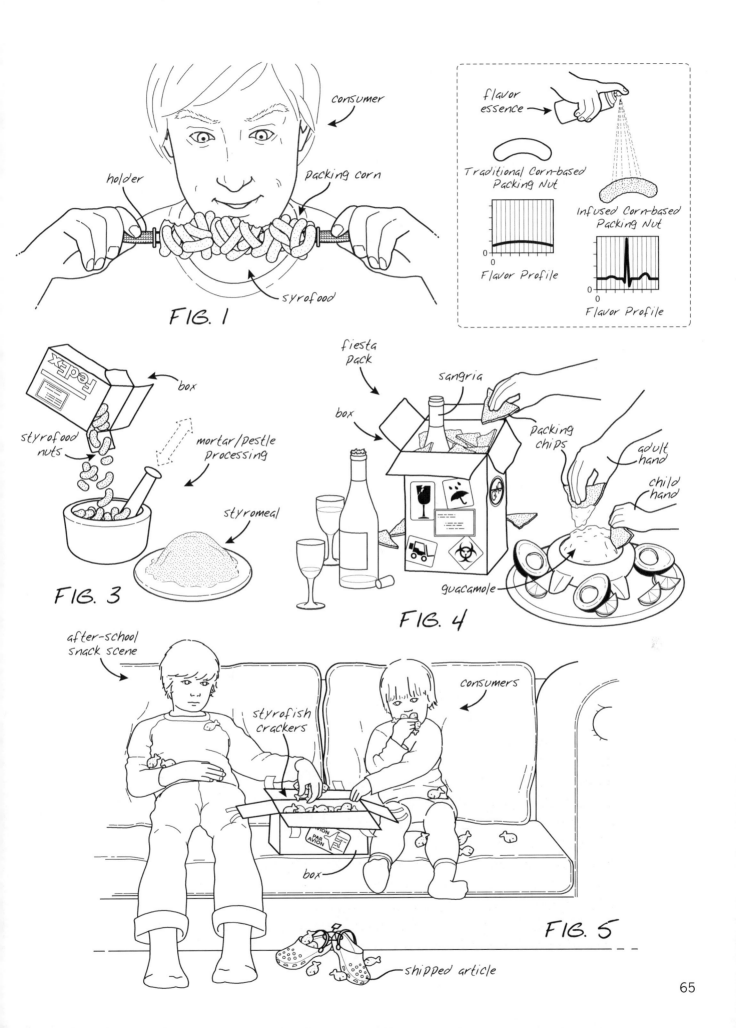

FIG. 1

consumer

holder

Packing corn

syrofood

flavor essence

Traditional Corn-based Packing Nut

Flavor Profile

0

Infused Corn-based Packing Nut

Flavor Profile

0

FIG. 3

box

styrofood nuts

mortar/pestle processing

styromeal

FIG. 4

fiesta pack

box

sangria

packing chips

adult hand

child hand

guacamole

FIG. 5

after-school snack scene

styrofish crackers

consumers

box

shipped article

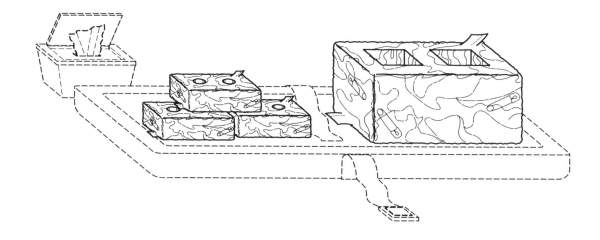

Diaper Brick

ABSTRACT
Brick-like building materials made from soiled diapers.

BACKGROUND OF INVENTION
Remodeling your home is now as easy—and natural—as filling a diaper.

We spend an inordinate amount of time and money removing soiled diapers from our homes. We individually wrap the diapers in plastic to keep their foul odor at bay. We buy expensive diaper bins to keep them out of sight. We even hire people to come and remove our bags of soiled diapers for us. Why not keep the diapers in the home and put them to good use? Why not treat them as free construction materials for remodeling or, better yet, building our homes?

The current invention keeps this valuable commodity in the home to be used as a building block for repairs and new construction. The soiled diaper is first pressed into a brick form. Liquid mortar mix is added and, once cured, the "brick" is removed from the form and ready for use. The Diaper Brick can be tinted to perfectly match traditional masonry. Or, if a marbled effect is desired, the diapers can be formed *au naturel*.

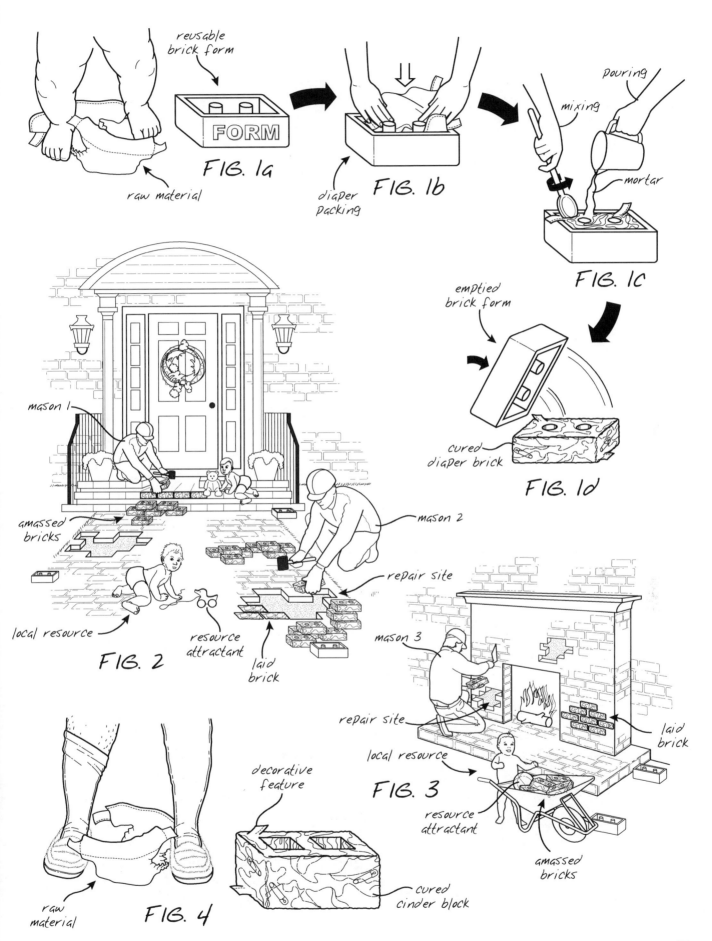

reusable brick form

raw material

FIG. 1a

diaper packing

FIG. 1b

pouring

mixing

mortar

FIG. 1c

emptied brick form

cured diaper brick

FIG. 1d

mason 1

amassed bricks

local resource

resource attractant

laid brick

FIG. 2

mason 2

repair site

mason 3

repair site

local resource

laid brick

FIG. 3

resource attractant

amassed bricks

decorative feature

cured cinder block

raw material

FIG. 4

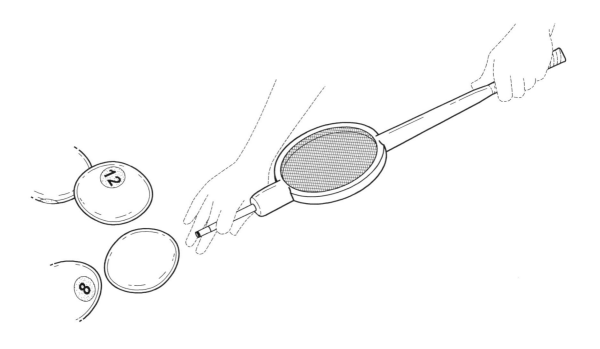

Sports Omniquipment

ABSTRACT

Standardized athletic equipment for engaging in a plurality of popular sporting events.

BACKGROUND OF INVENTION

Sinew, polyurethane, cowhide, old-growth hardwood, titanium, and polyester are among the least renewable, most carbon-exhaustive materials, and yet they are also the most widely used materials in athletic equipment. When one considers that there are 347 popular sports worldwide, each of which has its own unique equipment, one can appreciate the catastrophic consequences. In an effort to reduce Idle Stadium Syndrome, some municipalities have combined the playing areas of outdoor sports (e.g., a football/baseball stadium) and indoor sports (e.g., a basketball/hockey arena) into shared facilities. However, little effort has gone into combining the equipment used by athletes engaged in the different sports. Sadly, at the end of the season for "Sport A" the equipment is retired or discarded. And at that very moment, the start of the season for "Sport B," an entirely new set of equipment is manufactured and put into action.

The current invention seeks to reduce material waste by distilling the common features of popular sports gear into simplified, universal gear that is shared among athletes and used year-round. Subtle alterations to the rules and playing area may be required. Athletes could apply Orientation Appliques to the gear until they adjust to the new equipment shape.

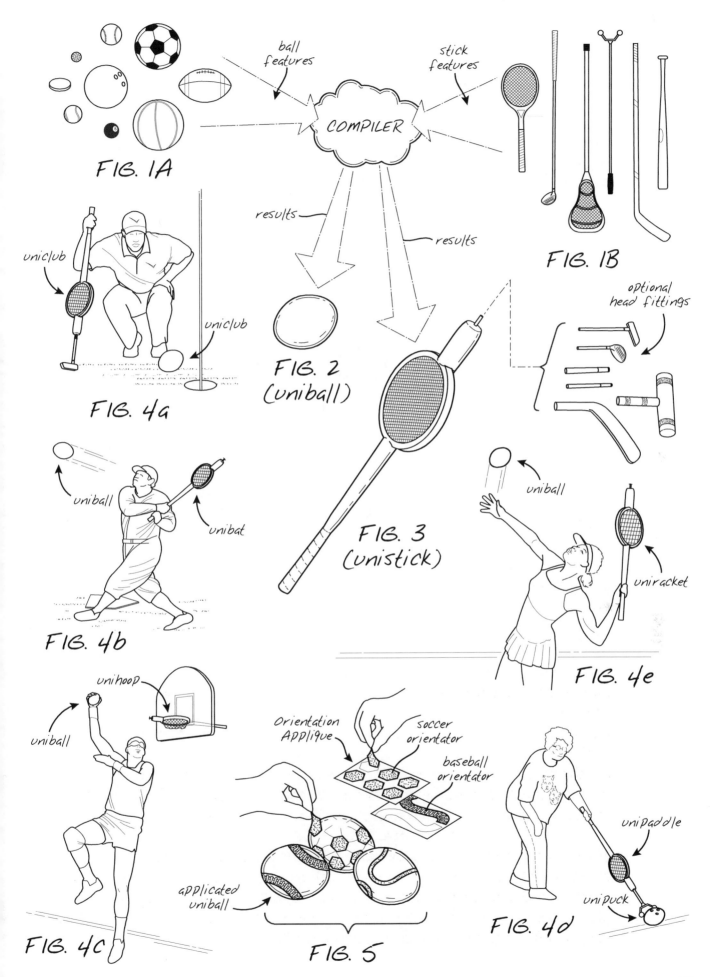

FIG. 1A

ball features

COMPILER

stick features

FIG. 1B

results

results

FIG. 2 (uniball)

FIG. 3 (unistick)

optional head fittings

uniclub

uniclub

FIG. 4a

uniball

unibat

FIG. 4b

uniball

uniracket

FIG. 4e

unihoop

uniball

FIG. 4c

Orientation Applique

soccer orientator

baseball orientator

applicated uniball

FIG. 5

unipaddle

unipuck

FIG. 4d

69

Coopicle

ABSTRACT

A cube-shaped enclosure inserted into empty cubicles and used to raise livestock for consumption and companionship.

BACKGROUND OF INVENTION

You know you should think globally, act locally, and consume sustainably. But who has time? Traditional 9-to-5 office workers now work 7:00 a.m. to 7:00 p.m. and barely make it home in time to watch their favorite shows. Tragically, these people find themselves eating two or three meals per day at fast-food restaurants and cafeterias, and from coin-operated vending machines. Besides the gastric consequences of this diet, the carbon footprint of processed food is among the highest on the planet. By one estimate, these foods travel as far as 1,300 MPO (miles per ounce) before being consumed.

The livestock cube shown here brings farm-fresh produce and meat right into the office with you, bringing new meaning to the idiom "What's on your plate?" A conduit extending from each enclosure to the roof removes manure from the Coopicle and disseminates it on the rooftop garden as fertilizer. The conduit could also house optical fibers if natural sunlight is appropriate for the enclosed animals. Farm odors could optionally be removed from the office via this same conduit.

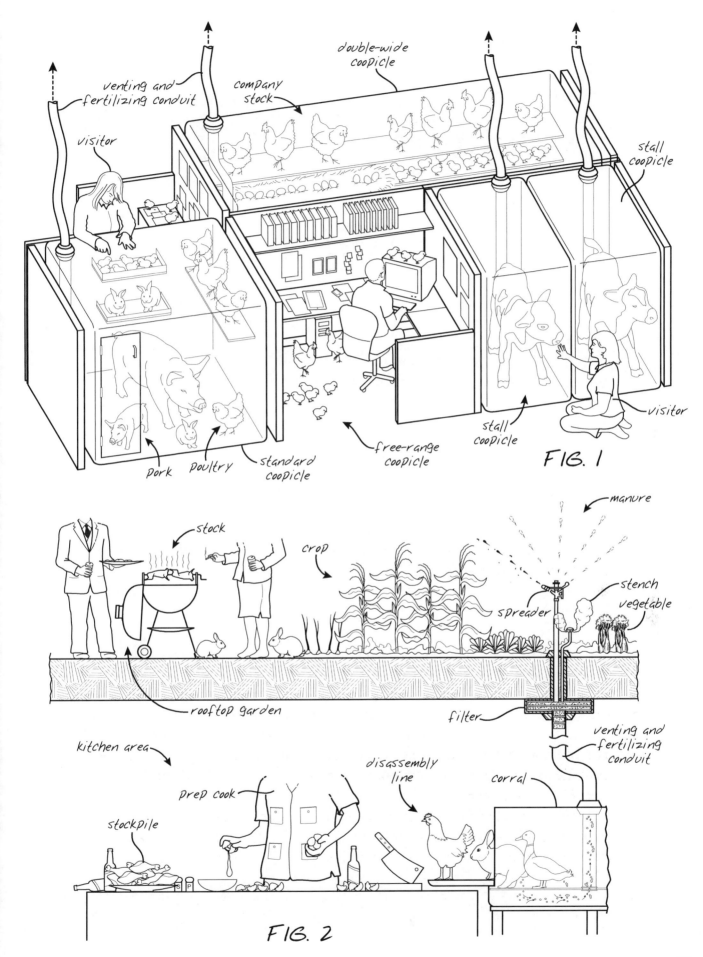

FIG. 1

venting and fertilizing conduit

visitor

company stock

double-wide coopicle

stall coopicle

visitor

Pork

Poultry

standard coopicle

free-range coopicle

stall coopicle

FIG. 2

manure

stock

crop

spreader

stench vegetable

rooftop garden

filter

venting and fertilizing conduit

corral

kitchen area

prep cook

disassembly line

stockpile

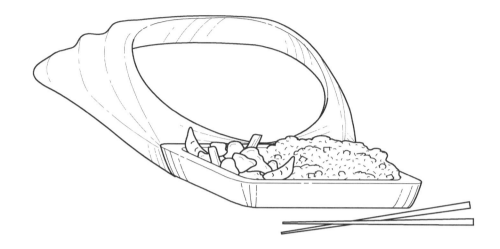

Carry-Out Scarf

ABSTRACT
A reusable container garment for transporting and serving take-out foods.

BACKGROUND OF INVENTION
There is no more room on our planet for take-out containers. Our ditches are filled. Our trash cans are overflowing. Our landfills are bursting. We need a reusable takeout container that fits so seamlessly into our lifestyles that we would never need to discard one again.

The current invention comprises a sturdy food trough integrated into scarf-like garments. Positioned around the neck, the reusable container conveniently holds one's meal close to one's face. Food debris that falls from the mouth or dribbles off the lips and chin is quickly returned to the receptacle for continued dining. The device virtually eliminates stained clothing and allows for extended wear and minimal laundering of shirts and slacks, thereby saving water. A petite embodiment of the scarf, The Snackscot, offers an elegant option for small meals and snacks.

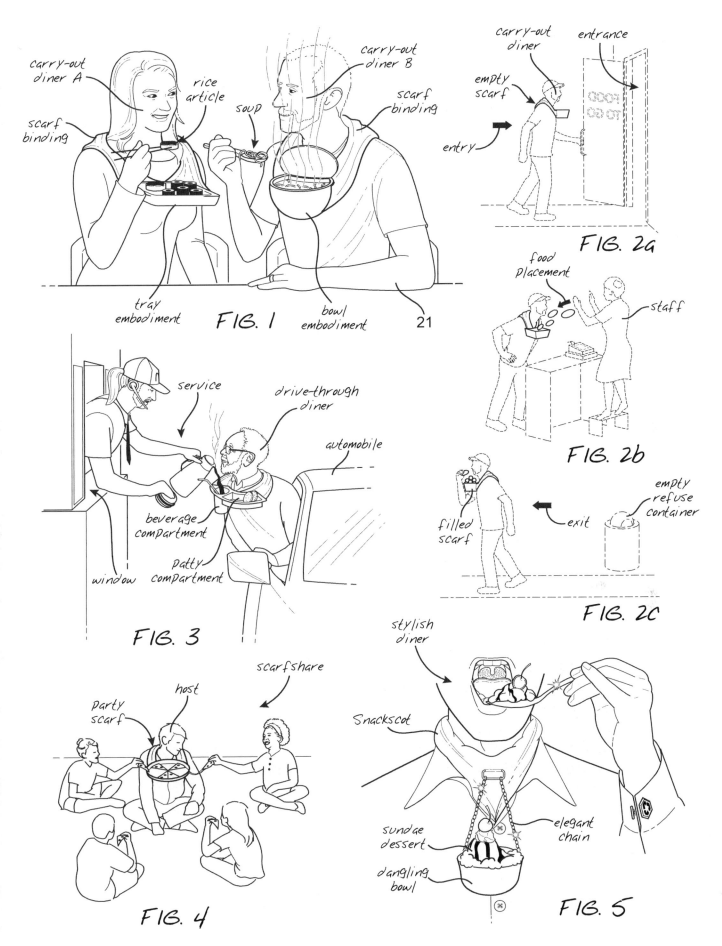

carry-out diner A

scarf binding

rice article

soup

carry-out diner B

scarf binding

tray embodiment

FIG. 1

bowl embodiment

21

carry-out diner

empty scarf

entry

entrance

FIG. 2a

food placement

staff

FIG. 2b

filled scarf

exit

empty refuse container

FIG. 2c

service

drive-through diner

automobile

beverage compartment

patty compartment

window

FIG. 3

party scarf

host

scarfshare

FIG. 4

stylish diner

Snackscot

sundae dessert

dangling bowl

elegant chain

FIG. 5

Chapter IV.
Solar

The days of stationary solar farms, installed in remote desert locations, will soon be a thing of the past. Today's solar cells—small, flexible, and ultraefficient—can be carried or worn everywhere you go. Their power can be used on the spot or uploaded to community energy banks.

The future of solar energy is almost unbearably bright.

SolarScreen

ABSTRACT
A sunscreen used for generating solar electric power.

BACKGROUND OF INVENTION
If your dermatologist jumped off of a bridge, would you jump, too?

For years, the medical establishment has been hounding us to use more sunscreen. The principles of sunscreen are simple and seemingly innocuous: a lotion containing small reflective particles is applied to the skin, where it deflects the sun's harmful rays away from the body. Unfortunately, sunscreen presents some serious health risks of its own. For instance, those rays that are reflected away from *your* body present serious health risks to *bystanders'* bodies by way of secondhand UV Exposure. Also, by reflecting the sun's hot rays back upward into the earth's atmosphere, your skin surface contributes to global warming and the slow demise of humankind.

Fortunately, the present invention employs a modified sunscreen that safely absorbs these hazardous rays and converts them into clean electricity. By replacing the sunscreen's reflective particles with nano solar panels, the sun's rays are safely captured and converted to electricity. And by substituting the sunscreen's lotion with electrically conductive fluid, the electrical charge is free to travel over the skin's surface until needed. AC/DC patches affixed to the body draw the electricity out of the SolarScreen, where the current can be used to operate local electronic devices and appliances. Insulated boots and gloves and a rubberized beach towel ensure safe application of this product.

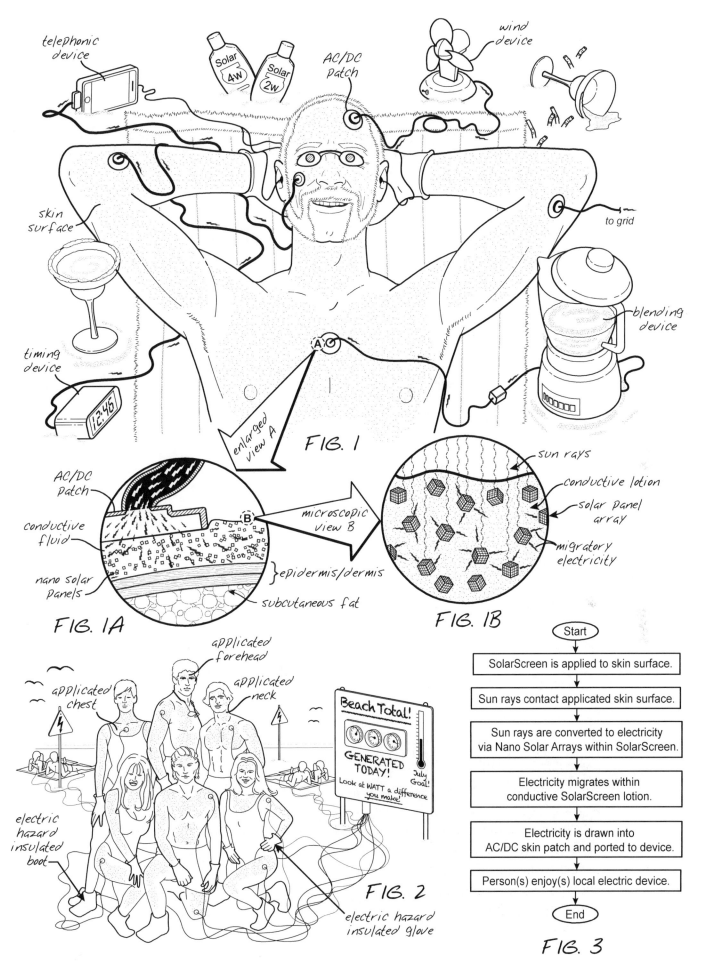

telephonic device

Solar 4w

Solar 2w

AC/DC Patch

wind device

skin surface

to grid

timing device

blending device

enlarged view A

FIG. 1

AC/DC Patch

conductive fluid

nano solar panels

epidermis/dermis

subcutaneous fat

FIG. 1A

microscopic view B

sun rays

conductive lotion

solar panel array

migratory electricity

FIG. 1B

applicated forehead

applicated chest

applicated neck

Beach Total!

GENERATED TODAY!

Look at WATT a difference you make!

July Goal!

electric hazard insulated boot

FIG. 2

electric hazard insulated glove

Start

SolarScreen is applied to skin surface.

Sun rays contact applicated skin surface.

Sun rays are converted to electricity via Nano Solar Arrays within SolarScreen.

Electricity migrates within conductive SolarScreen lotion.

Electricity is drawn into AC/DC skin patch and ported to device.

Person(s) enjoy(s) local electric device.

End

FIG. 3

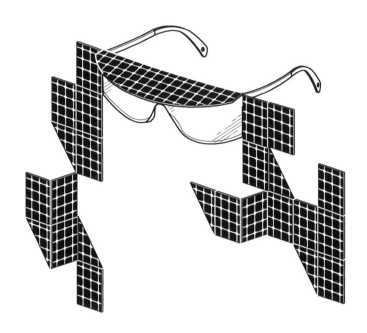

Solarglasses

ABSTRACT
A device worn on or around the face and head that provides
sun protection and solar electricity.

BACKGROUND OF INVENTION
Ray-Ban®. Louis Vuitton®. Oakley®: the sunglasses you wear say everything about you. Wouldn't it be nice to have a pair of shades that clearly say **I♥EARTH**?

Most likely, you wear your sunglasses when it is sunny. Coincidentally, solar panels are most effective when it is sunny. The current invention is a marriage between these two sun-dependent articles. Solar cells attached to sunglasses frames will provide clean electricity when exposed to sunlight. Additionally, the solar panels can extend beyond the traditional boundaries of sunglasses to increase the panel surface and offer attractive adornment. The sunglasses will command attention for their obvious devotion to earth and their striking design.

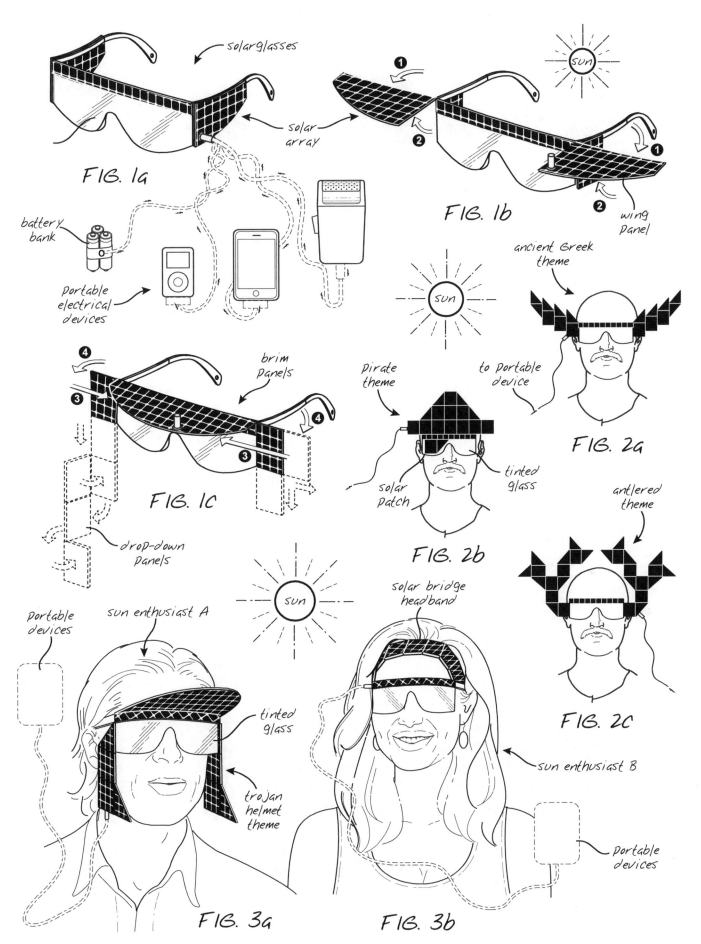

FIG. 1a — solarglasses — solar array

FIG. 1b — sun — wing panel

battery bank — Portable electrical devices

FIG. 1c — brim panels — drop-down panels

pirate theme — solar patch — tinted glass — FIG. 2b — sun

ancient Greek theme — to portable device — FIG. 2a

antlered theme — FIG. 2c

Portable devices — sun enthusiast A — sun — solar bridge headband — tinted glass — trojan helmet theme — FIG. 3a — FIG. 3b — sun enthusiast B — Portable devices

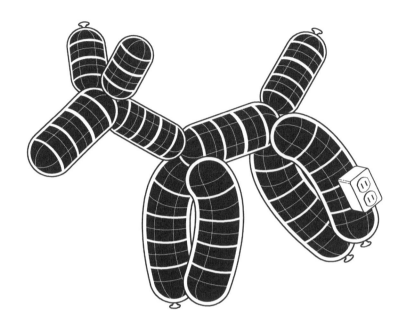

Cap 'n' Trap 'n' Trade

ABSTRACT
A method and device for trapping CO_2 emissions and creating solar electricity.

BACKGROUND OF INVENTION
We are all familiar with the controversial policy of cap and trade: "Company A" is allowed to pollute *more* by buying the rights from "Company B" (a company that pollutes *less*). Many complain that the policy does nothing to reduce carbon dioxide emissions. Unfortunately, we humans will continue to emit CO_2 until there is a paradigm shift in energy policy. Until then, our best option is to Cap 'n' Trap 'n' Trade.

With the current invention, we first place a "cap" on mufflers, chimneys, and smokestacks, either manually or with aid of robotics. This cap, made of latex and coated with flexible solar panels, should be colorful and/or of whimsical design. Next, we "trap" noxious CO_2 within this inflatable prophylactic.

Finally, we "trade" haze, smog, and acid rain clouds for bright, playful, solar balloons that create clean electricity as they bounce across our planet.

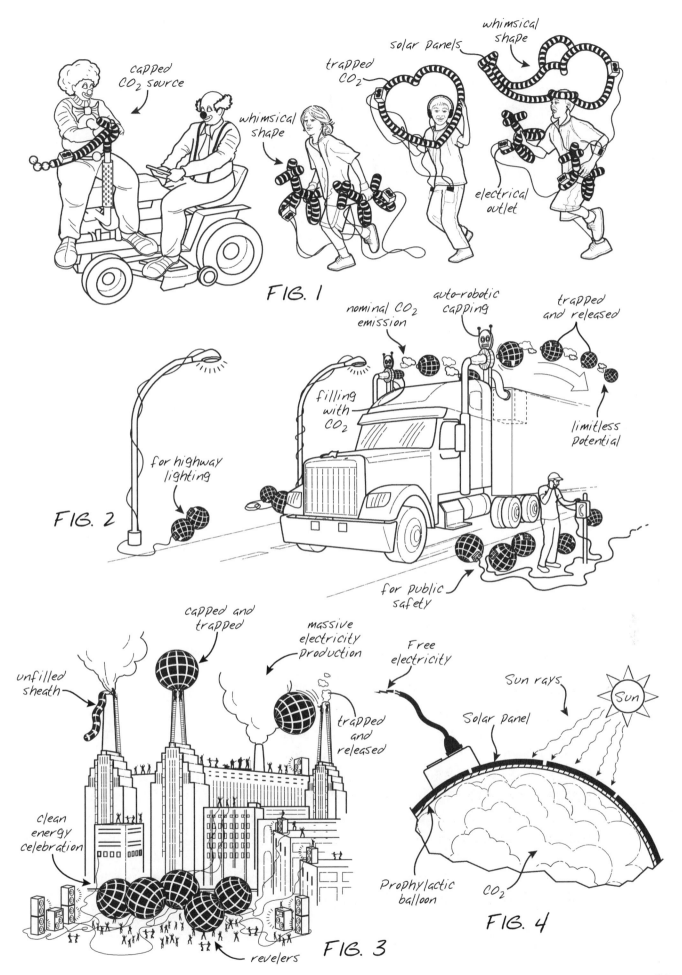

FIG. 1

FIG. 2

FIG. 3

FIG. 4

E•ccoutrement

ABSTRACT

A passive method for generating electricity while sunbathing and recreating.

BACKGROUND OF INVENTION

Scientists have calculated that if every beach on earth were covered with solar panels, we could generate enough electricity to power the planet. Making this a reality could be a walk on the beach.

Visit any popular waterfront during the summer months and you may notice a large amount of exposed skin surface area. More noticeable, though, is the impressive amount of exposed *non-skin* surface area: hats, umbrellas, towels, swimsuits, books, etc. Skin and non-skin surfaces absorb the sun's rays equally. But until now, only the skin surfaces utilized the rays—turning darker and making you look more desirable. Non-skin surfaces have simply been wasting the sun's rays. The current invention creates energy-generating workhorses from beach accoutrements and paraphernalia. By using micro solar cells to encase, inlay, and bejewel every non-skin surface available, we can provide ample electricity to power the beachfront and beyond.

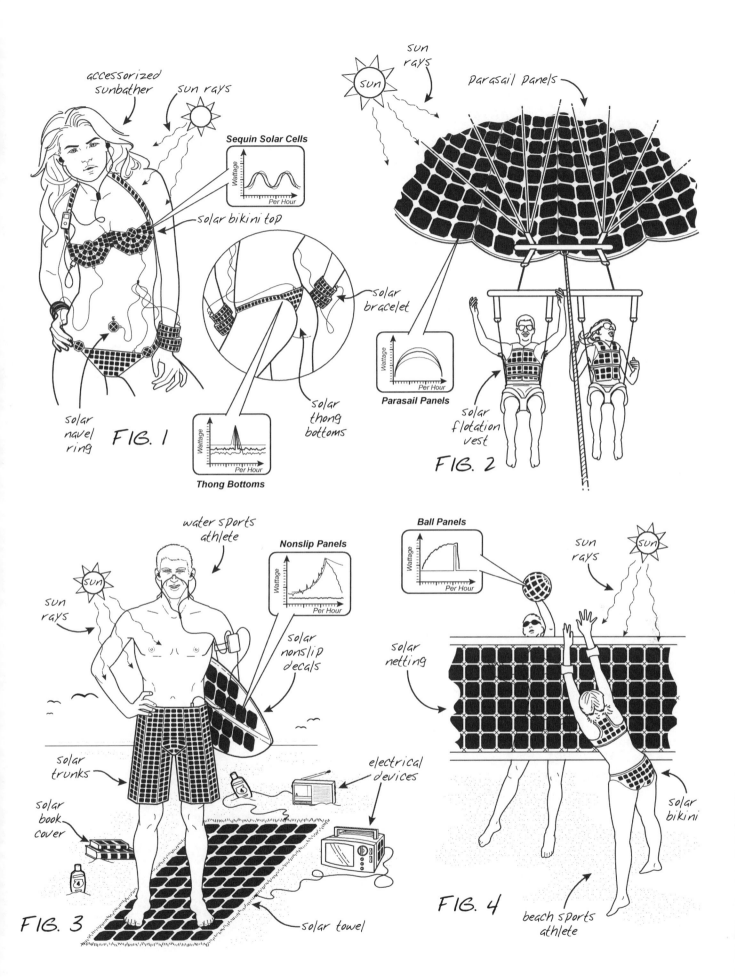

FIG. 1

accessorized sunbather

sun rays

Sequin Solar Cells

Wattage / Per Hour

solar bikini top

solar bracelet

solar navel ring

solar thong bottoms

Wattage / Per Hour

Thong Bottoms

FIG. 2

sun rays

sun

Parasail Panels

Wattage / Per Hour

Parasail Panels

solar flotation vest

FIG. 3

water sports athlete

sun

sun rays

Nonslip Panels

Wattage / Per Hour

solar nonslip decals

solar trunks

solar book cover

electrical devices

solar towel

FIG. 4

Ball Panels

Wattage / Per Hour

sun rays

sun

solar netting

solar bikini

beach sports athlete

Chapter V.
Wind

Wind energy is abundant not only in the sky.
Manmade wind is all around us. We create wind with our cars,
our bikes, and with our own bodies.

Man makes wind, and man should also harness it.

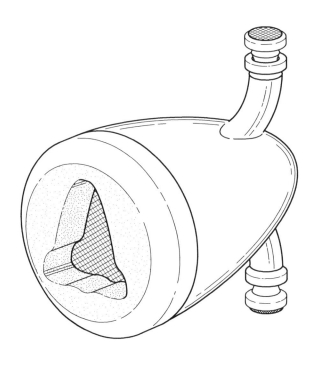

Sneeze Cone

ABSTRACT

A conically shaped electrical generator driven by the high-velocity blast of a sneeze. The device could be operated manually or chin actuated.

BACKGROUND OF INVENTION

For nearly six decades, scientists have been trying to harness the high winds of hurricanes to make electricity. By one estimate, the wattage generated by a single Category 2 hurricane would provide one year's worth of electricity for a city the size of Cincinnati. To date, however, the high winds these scientists seek have torn to bits every windmill, turbine, generator, and wind sock that has been erected. Unbeknownst to them, an easier and less destructive alternative sat right under their noses: the 150 to 200 mph winds of a human sneeze dwarf those of any hurricane. Though less sustained than hurricane winds, sneeze gusts drive turbine blades with unbelievable force. In the current invention, small electrical generators capture sneeze winds and create electricity for personal use or for upload to the grid. During peak allergy seasons, sufferers could be recruited to sneeze farms for camaraderie and profit.

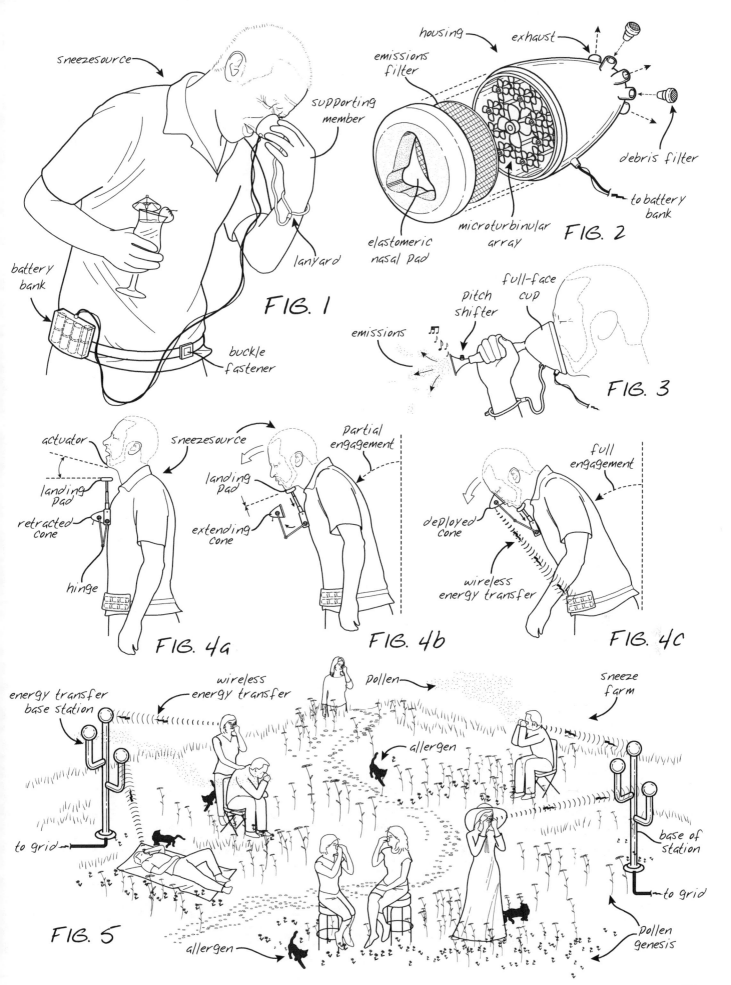

FIG. 1

sneezesource

supporting member

lanyard

battery bank

buckle fastener

FIG. 2

housing

exhaust

emissions filter

debris filter

to battery bank

elastomeric nasal pad

microturbinular array

FIG. 3

pitch shifter

full-face cup

emissions

FIG. 4a

actuator

sneezesource

landing pad

retracted cone

hinge

FIG. 4b

partial engagement

landing pad

extending cone

FIG. 4c

full engagement

deployed cone

wireless energy transfer

FIG. 5

energy transfer base station

wireless energy transfer

pollen

sneeze farm

allergen

to grid

allergen

base of station

to grid

pollen genesis

87

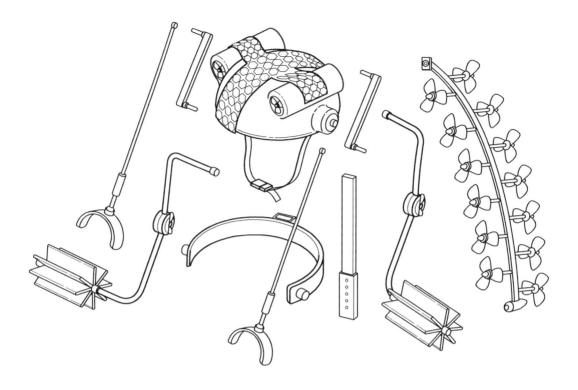

Hybrid Helmet

ABSTRACT

A bicycling helmet with variety of alternative-energy technologies attached thereto.

BACKGROUND OF INVENTION

Scientists need to step out of the lab and go for a nice bike ride. Research into bike-driven electrical generators has always been conducted in laboratories, using stationary bikes, and has focused solely on the pedaling mechanism. But from a holistic perspective, the bicycle is so much more than a simple pedaling machine. Sadly, science has overlooked the quintessential experience of bicycling that lends itself perfectly to expanded electricity generation: riding in the glorious morning sun with an exhilarating breeze flowing over your body, the hiss of smooth tires on the hot pavement below, flaunting your impressive gear to fellow cyclists.

The invention disclosed here integrates solar panels, vortex chambers, a slipstream turbine, a paddlewheel generator, and a knee-thrust crankshaft. When worn on the helmet like the stunning antlers of a trophy stag, there will be no question about one's tech prowess.

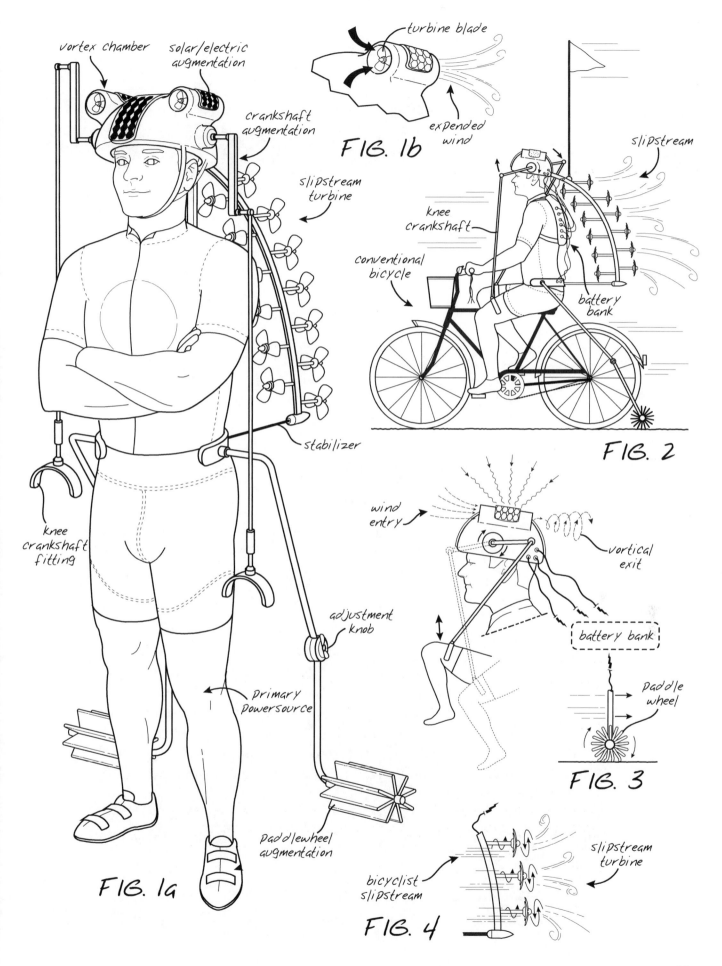

vortex chamber

solar/electric augmentation

crankshaft augmentation

slipstream turbine

stabilizer

knee crankshaft fitting

Primary Powersource

adjustment knob

Paddlewheel augmentation

FIG. 1a

turbine blade

expended wind

FIG. 1b

slipstream

knee crankshaft

conventional bicycle

battery bank

FIG. 2

wind entry

vortical exit

battery bank

Paddle wheel

FIG. 3

bicyclist slipstream

slipstream turbine

FIG. 4

Cig•O•Watt

ABSTRACT
A method and apparatus for smokers to provide free electrical utilities to the public through inhalation-powered electric generators.

BACKGROUND OF INVENTION
Tobacco enthusiasts have been demonized since the 1980s, when scientists concluded that smoking kills smokers, their families, and bystanders. Smokers feared they would continue to be marginalized in society until tobacco became banned altogether. But with the following invention, smokers will be welcomed back into their communities and encouraged to smoke with abandon for the public good. The device, when loaded with the butt end of a cigarette and placed in one's mouth, offers two unique ways to generate electricity: inhaling and exhaling. The apparatus requires deep, vigorous breathing to force smoke through a myriad of microturbine blades, thereby strengthening the lungs and slightly improving the health of smokers. An optional wattage meter on the barrel of the generator measures electrical output and could be used in competitions that reward citizens for generating this free public utility.

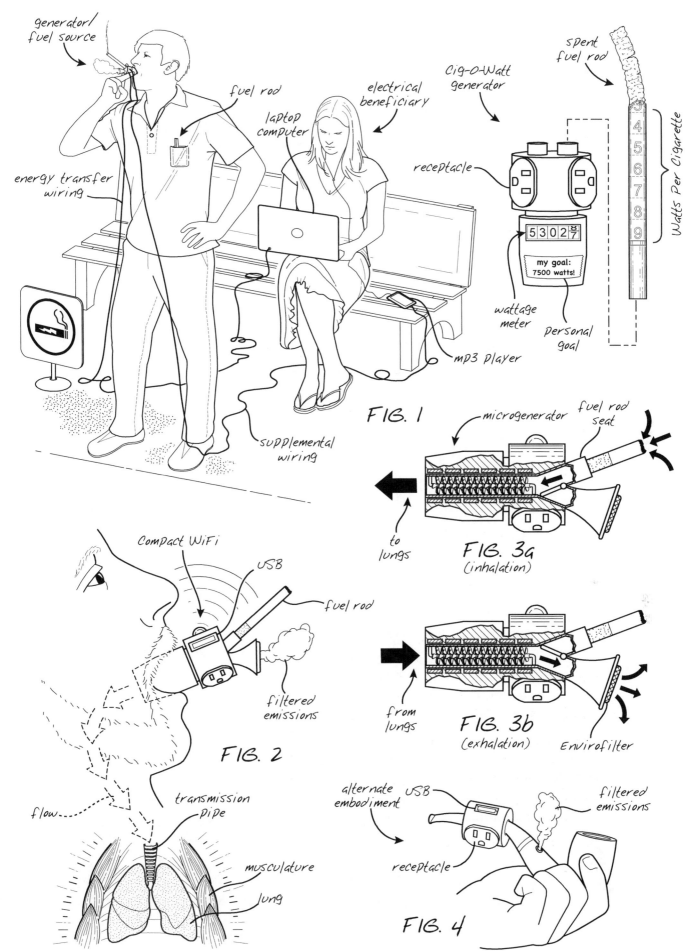

generator/fuel source

fuel rod

laptop computer

electrical beneficiary

Cig-O-Watt generator

spent fuel rod

receptacle

energy transfer wiring

Watts Per Cigarette

5302 7

my goal: 7500 watts!

wattage meter

personal goal

supplemental wiring

mp3 player

FIG. 1

Compact WiFi

USB

fuel rod

microgenerator

fuel rod seat

filtered emissions

FIG. 2

to lungs

FIG. 3a
(inhalation)

from lungs

FIG. 3b
(exhalation)

Envirofilter

flow

transmission pipe

alternate embodiment

USB

filtered emissions

receptacle

musculature

lung

FIG. 4

The Commuter Sail

ABSTRACT

A lightweight commuter vehicle powered by vehicular winds.

BACKGROUND OF INVENTION

Consider wind energy for a moment.

You're probably imagining the clean, powerful gales that roll down from mountaintops and across our oceans, driving turbine blades and creating renewable electricity. Well, researchers have recently discovered an over-looked wind source that, although malodorous and occasionally toxic, is *very* abundant: the automotive jet stream found alongside every busy highway in the world. These winds don't have the strength to drive a turbine, but, as anyone waiting for a tow truck alongside the highway will attest, they are forceful enough to push you around.

The current invention offers a zero-emission vehicle that can be used to carry commuters down highway shoulders. Large sheets of sailcloth, held by the rider or integrated into a travel suit, catch the jet stream generated by high-way vehicles. The commuter is propelled briskly down the highway on an all-terrain wheeled chassis. Stability features could be mounted to the chassis to prevent falling and injury. An optional breathing apparatus can be deployed to prevent respiratory complications from carbon monoxide exposure.

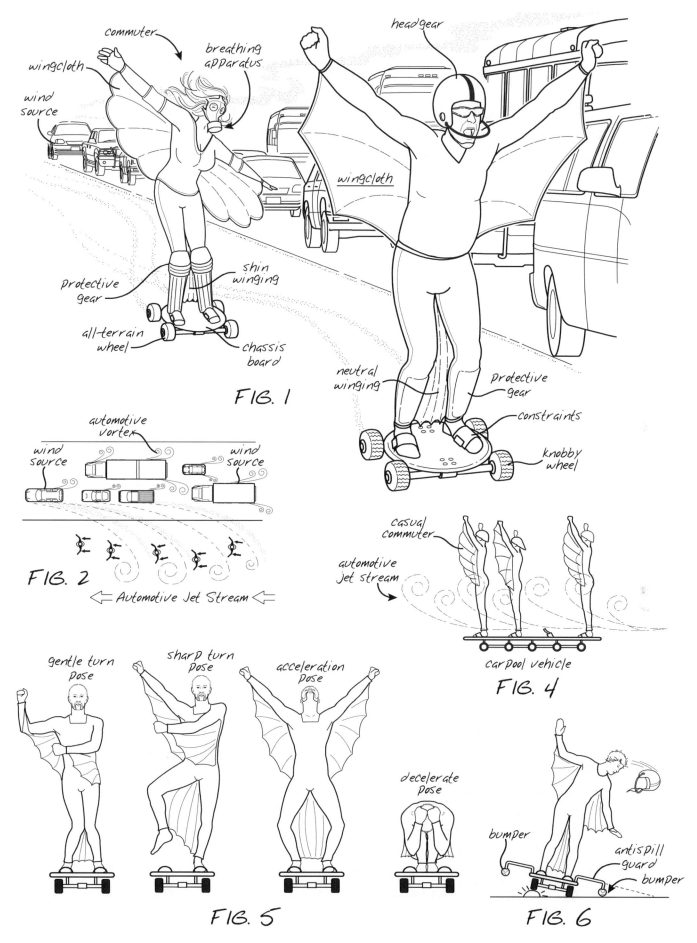

FIG. 1

commuter

breathing apparatus

wingcloth

wind source

headgear

wingcloth

Protective gear

shin winging

all-terrain wheel

chassis board

neutral winging

Protective gear

constraints

knobby wheel

FIG. 2

automotive vortex

wind source

wind source

← Automotive Jet Stream ←

casual commuter

automotive jet stream

carpool vehicle

FIG. 4

gentle turn Pose

sharp turn Pose

acceleration Pose

decelerate Pose

bumper

antispill guard bumper

FIG. 5

FIG. 6

Chapter VI.
Water

The close proximity of our faucets to our drains speaks volumes about our lack of respect for water—we treat water like it's disposable. In less than a second, tap water goes from a resource of limitless potential to sewer water. It's time we focus on providing water the fulfilling midlife that it deserves.

Here are some ways of keeping our most valuable resource from simply going down the drain.

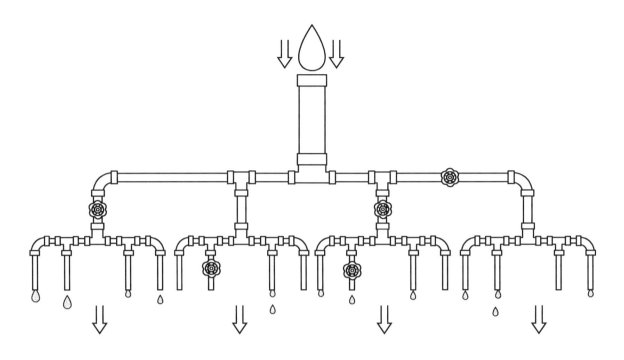

Trickle-Down Water Conservation

ABSTRACT
A method for repurposing water in an apartment building.

BACKGROUND OF INVENTION
Gravity: it's been keeping the cosmos running smoothly since the dawn of time. It keeps planets aligned and stars from falling. It pulls rain down from the clouds and streams down from the mountains. Years ago, the Romans put it to work in their aqueducts, but, sadly, since the advent of modern machinery, man has lost touch with this fundamental force. Yet gravity is free, abundant, perfectly clean, and quietly waiting for us to employ it.

The current invention provides a system for gravitationally fed water conservation. The top unit of an apartment building is supplied with copious volumes of heated water that is used at the occupant's leisure. The excess is pulled downward gravitationally through modified plumbing and an optional filtration system. The occupants of lower units, having scheduled their bathing sessions to correspond with those of the upper unit's occupant, will benefit from the heated and pre-lathered water that pours over them. The occupant of the upper unit is encouraged to practice altruism by bathing regularly.

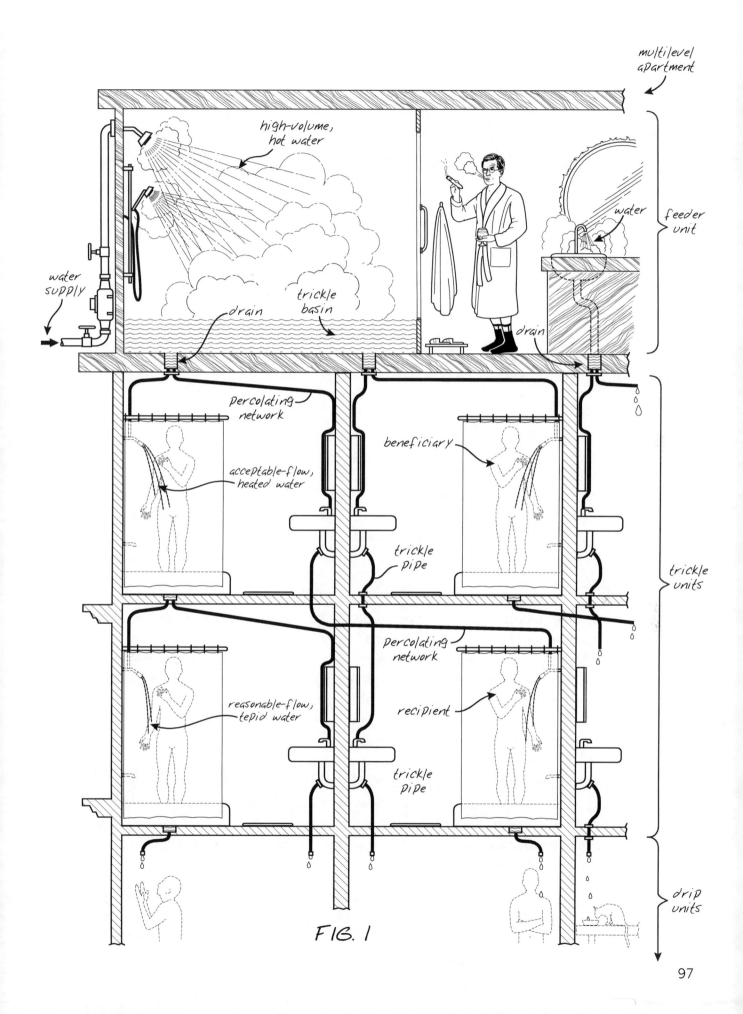

multilevel
apartment

high-volume,
hot water

water

feeder
unit

water
supply

drain

trickle
basin

drain

percolating
network

beneficiary

acceptable-flow,
heated water

trickle
pipe

trickle
units

percolating
network

reasonable-flow,
tepid water

recipient

trickle
pipe

drip
units

FIG. 1

97

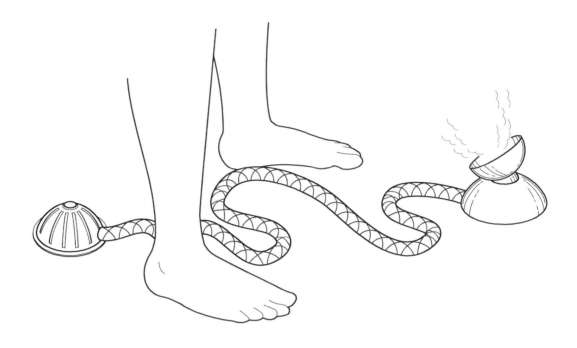

Shower Viper

ABSTRACT

A device for reclaiming, filtering, and redirecting used, and otherwise discarded, shower water toward problematic regions of the human body during a shower. Optional attachments provide customizability of redirected stream.

BACKGROUND OF INVENTION

Due to an increasing number of droughts, state and local officials have been forced to impose water restrictions nationwide. In many areas, shower rationing is now common and under strict enforcement. To comply with the restrictions, people who bathe are required to either shorten their showers or use a flow-regulating showerhead to reduce water usage. These methods leave the bather both disappointed with the experience and, often, feeling a general lack of cleanliness in their under regions.

The present invention employs a pump and ionic crystal filtration system to partially clean, recirculate, and redirect the used shower water to provide complete water coverage. The unit might also include a high-efficiency water heater to allow for extended or even perpetual showering sessions using as little as one quart of water.

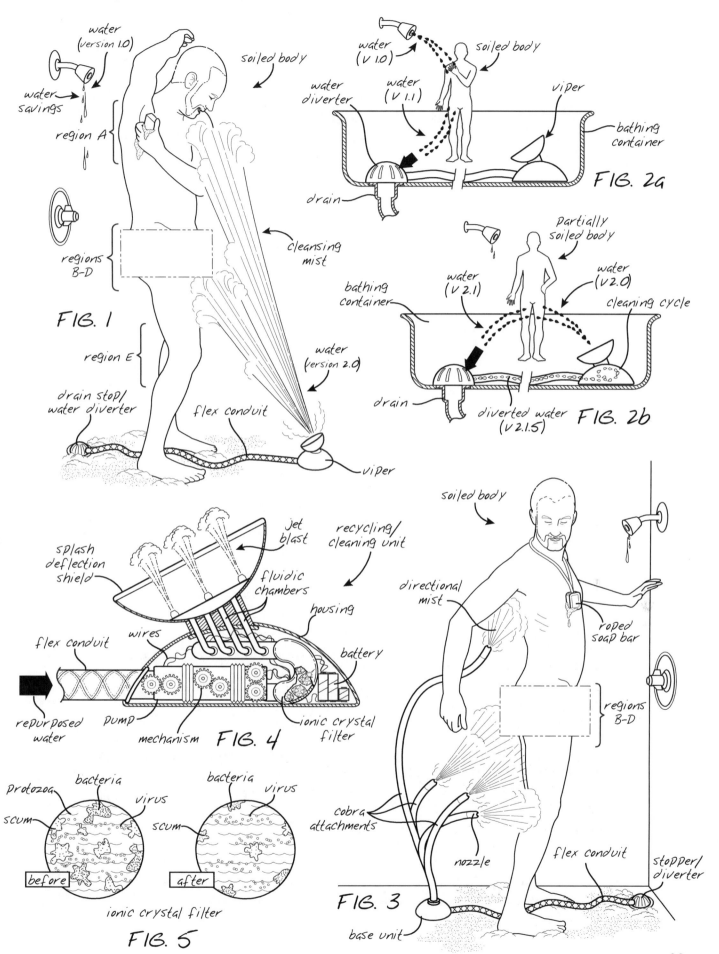

FIG. 1

water (version 1.0)
water savings
soiled body
region A
regions B-D
cleansing mist
region E
drain stop/ water diverter
flex conduit
water (version 2.0)
viper

FIG. 2a

water (v 1.0)
soiled body
water diverter
water (v 1.1)
viper
bathing container
drain

FIG. 2b

partially soiled body
water (v 2.1)
water (v 2.0)
bathing container
cleaning cycle
drain
diverted water (v 2.1.5)

FIG. 4

splash deflection shield
jet blast
recycling/ cleaning unit
fluidic chambers
housing
flex conduit
wires
battery
repurposed water
pump
mechanism
ionic crystal filter

FIG. 5

protozoa
bacteria
virus
scum
before
bacteria
virus
scum
after
ionic crystal filter

FIG. 3

soiled body
directional mist
roped soap bar
regions B-D
cobra attachments
nozzle
flex conduit
stopper/ diverter
base unit

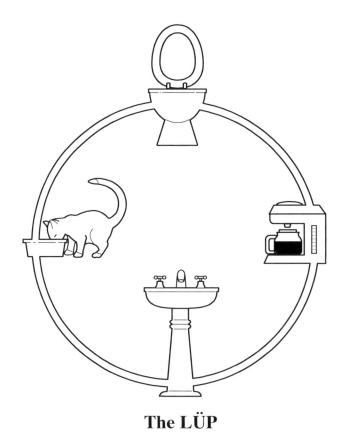

The LÜP

ABSTRACT
Devices and method for recycling water ad infinitum in the home.

BACKGROUND OF INVENTION
Washing your dishes with toilet water? Brewing coffee from bathwater? Some would call this loopy. I would call this The LÜP.

The earth's biosphere is masterful at conserving water. It hasn't lost a drop in over 20 billion years. Rainwater becomes runoff that feeds rivers and streams. Rivers and streams feed lakes and oceans where water evaporates into clouds. Clouds drop snow onto our polar caps, creating glaciers that store frozen water. With running water becoming increasingly scarce across our parched planet, it seems only natural that we now turn to nature's perfect model for water conservation.

The current invention comprises a closed-circuit system of water reclamation. Like nature's model, the water in this circuit is transformed into the three different states (solid, liquid, gas) as it passes through the home. A standard charcoal filtration system should adequately remove dangerous particles from the water and guarantee safe consumption. Foreign contamination of the water can be further avoided by preventing foreign bodies (insects, animals, people) from entering the LÜP-osphere. Parcels of groceries and clothing can be delivered to a decontamination chamber before they enter the LÜP-osphere.

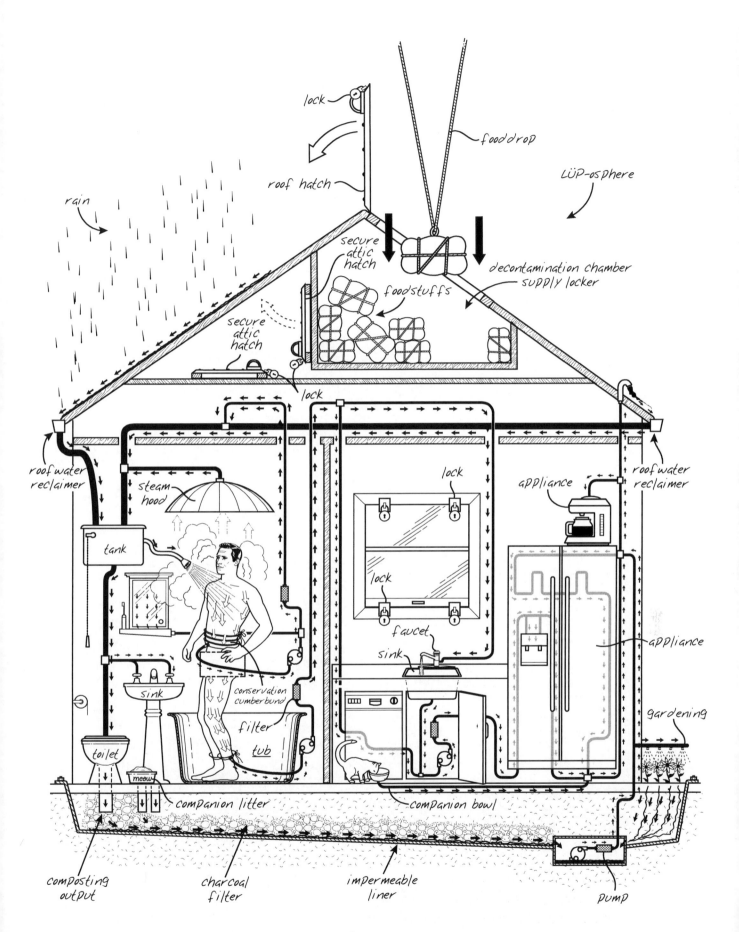

FIG. 1

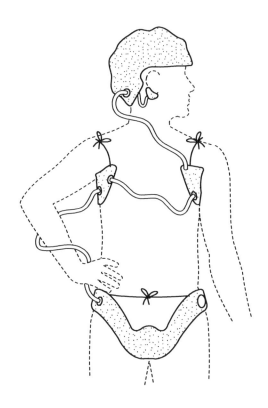

Dishower

ABSTRACT

Device and method for cleansing regions of the human body with dishwasher water.

BACKGROUND OF INVENTION

Residential dishwashers use up to 20 gallons of heated water per cycle, roughly the same amount of heated water used during a shower. Dishwashers use soap detergents to clean and sanitize dinnerware, similar to the cleaning process used to clean bodies in most showers around the world. With water conservation on everyone's mind, we begin to see these coincidences for what they truly are: opportunities.

Using reclaimed water from the dishwasher, the current invention offers a portable method for cleaning areas of the human body that require frequent washing. After removing filth, discarded hair, and sloughed skin from the body, this device forwards the waste back into the dishwasher and on to the garbage disposal for pulverizing. Mild dishwashing detergent will cleanse dishes and bodies alike in a reasonably safe manner. Since the cleansing cycle may take slightly longer than a typical shower, the freedom of movement offered by the cleansing pouches and lengthy hoses allows one to engage in a variety of activities in and around the kitchen during the cleansing process.

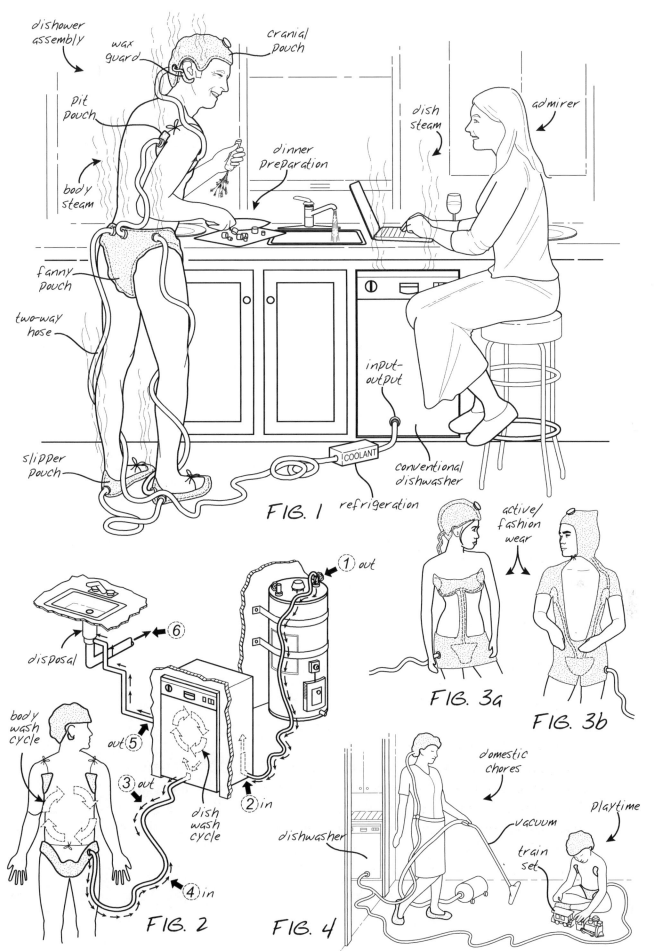

dishower assembly

wax guard

cranial pouch

pit pouch

dish steam

admirer

body steam

dinner preparation

fanny pouch

two-way hose

input-output

slipper pouch

COOLANT

conventional dishwasher

refrigeration

FIG. 1

① out

disposal

⑥

body wash cycle

out ⑤

③ out

② in

dish wash cycle

④ in

FIG. 2

active/fashion wear

FIG. 3a

FIG. 3b

domestic chores

vacuum

playtime

dishwasher

train set

FIG. 4

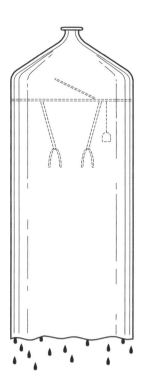

Irrigation Shower

ABSTRACT
A device and method for repurposing shower water in a horticultural setting.

BACKGROUND OF INVENTION
In these days of global warming and drought, a lush, green garden has become a symbol of water abuse and gluttony. A wilted, brown garden, on the other hand, is a veritable badge of environmentalism—*brown* is the new *green*.

But as plants die, CO_2 levels rise, leading to global warming. It's a vicious circle. We grapple with our water dilemma each morning as we shower, feeling like selfish hypocrites. Do we deserve a daily shower in our homes while our gardens perish in the out-of-doors?

Now, you and your flora can shower together.

The present invention is a mobile irrigating shower tent. A water basin at the top of the unit is filled with traditional shower water. The loaded tent is then walked to a garden area where the water is released onto the body of a user. The runoff water is directed outside of the tent and onto the surrounding garden through a multiplicity of means.

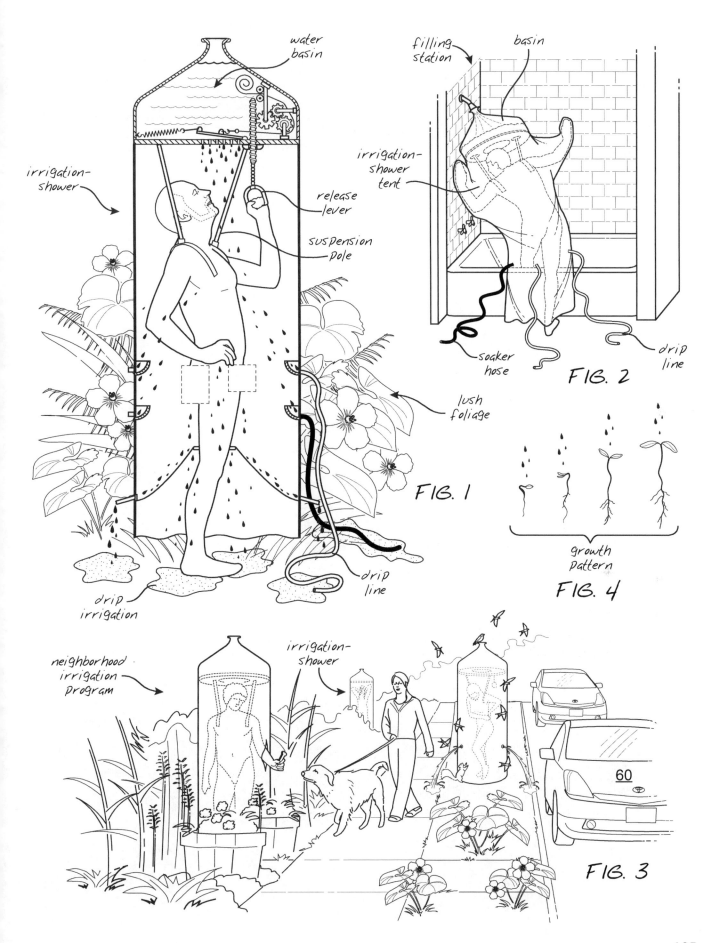

water basin

irrigation-shower

release lever

suspension pole

drip irrigation

drip line

FIG. 1

filling station

basin

irrigation-shower tent

soaker hose

drip line

lush foliage

FIG. 2

growth pattern

FIG. 4

neighborhood irrigation program

irrigation-shower

60

FIG. 3

Chapter VII.
Emissions

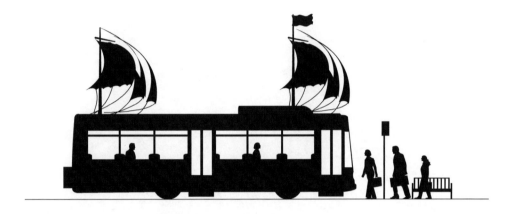

As a child I travelled with zero emissions: tricycle, bicycle, roller skates. Sadly, I now drive a gas-powered vehicle. The convenience of gas is undeniable, but the ideals of zero-emission travel should never be forgotten.

Here are inventions that find some middle ground.

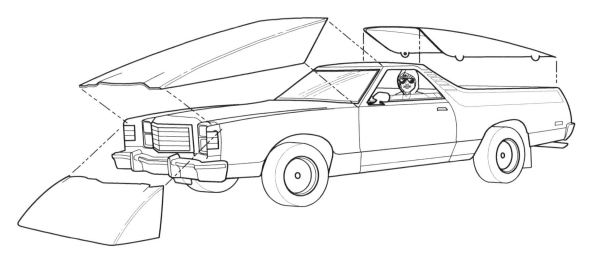

The Aeromerican Shield

ABSTRACT
Aerodynamic panels applied to automobiles for improved gas mileage, lower emissions, and greater camaraderie on roadways.

BACKGROUND OF INVENTION
The United States has become a deeply divided nation. Politically, socially, economically, and now, even automotively.

On one side of the automotive divide you'll find proud, hardworking men and women who love their American-made cars. On the other side of this divide you'll find earth-loving, conscientious people who demand fuel economy. For years the two sides simply agreed to disagree about vehicle choice. But as gas prices began to rise, the disagreement became volatile. One side became smug and self-righteous and started aggressively proselytizing fuel economy. The other side became defensive and resentful and struggled to control their road rage. Recent spikes in fuel prices have led many analysts to predict that this chasm will only continue to grow wider—that our country will literally be *driven* into crisis by our cars.

The current invention aims to bring "MPG Equality" to all Americans and begin reunifying our country. Aerodynamic panels are affixed to the wind-resistant contours of an auto body, thereby masking these areas from wind drag and increasing fuel efficiency. Furthermore, when all automobiles have uniformity of body shape, there will be less rivalry, coveting, and auto theft.

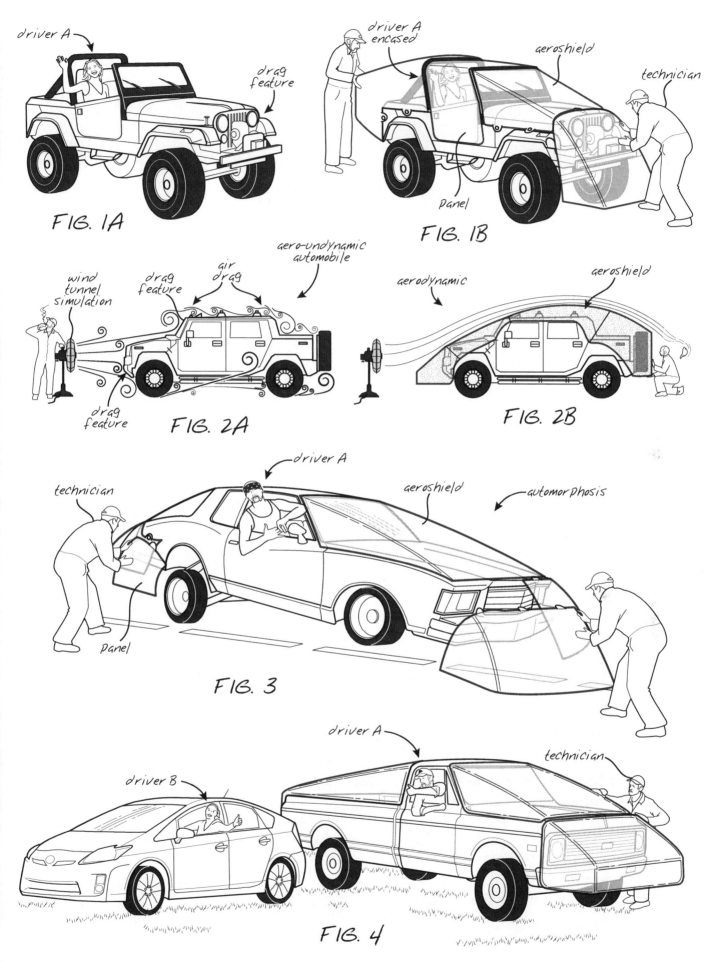

driver A

drag feature

FIG. 1A

driver A encased

aeroshield

technician

Panel

FIG. 1B

wind tunnel simulation

drag feature

air drag

aero-undynamic automobile

drag feature

FIG. 2A

aerodynamic

aeroshield

FIG. 2B

technician

driver A

aeroshield

automorphosis

Panel

FIG. 3

driver A

driver B

technician

FIG. 4

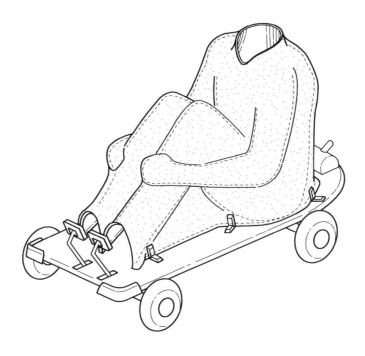

Person Car

ABSTRACT

An ultralight hybrid vehicle comprising a custom fiberglass body, a corn resin chassis, a titanium pedal-steering system, and a high-efficiency engine.

BACKGROUND OF INVENTION

Cars are heavy. They burn an enormous amount of petroleum fuel. They require an unfathomable amount of energy and resources to manufacture. Cars wreak havoc on passengers and pedestrians during a collision. But we love our cars. They offer utility, transportation, and a sense of freedom. Cars bolster social status and can even provide companionship. They are statements about who we are and what we aspire to be. Cars will always be with us.

The current invention allows our love affair with cars to safely continue via a light, ecologically sound, carbon-sensitive automobile. The ultralight weight of this vehicle makes it well suited to alternative energy sources like wind, solar, or Homeopatholine engines. The body style of this automobile can be endlessly customized to meet one's needs.

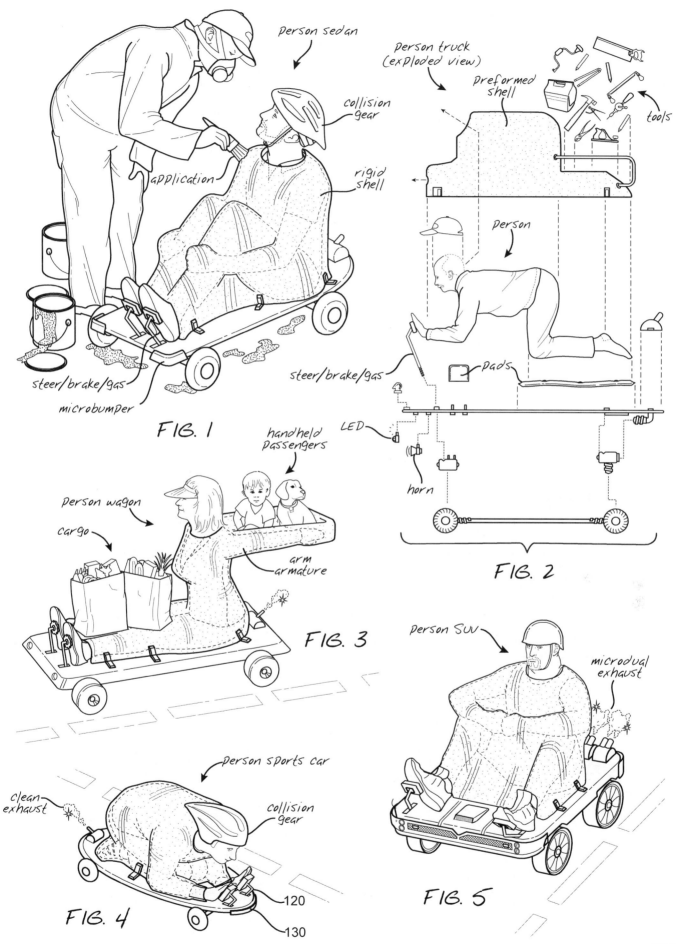

Person sedan

collision gear

rigid shell

application

steer/brake/gas

microbumper

FIG. 1

Person truck (exploded view)

Preformed shell

tools

Person

steer/brake/gas

pads

LED

horn

FIG. 2

handheld Passengers

Person wagon

cargo

arm armature

FIG. 3

Person SUV

microdual exhaust

FIG. 5

Person sports car

clean exhaust

collision gear

120

130

FIG. 4

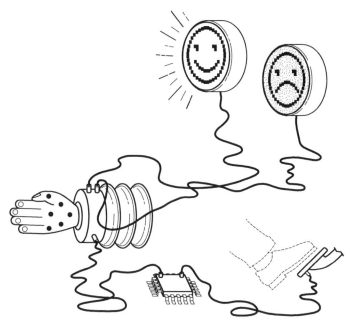

Bumper Buddy

ABSTRACT

A device that allows two or more motorized vehicles to form a hands-free, cruise-controlled network.

BACKGROUND OF INVENTION

If someone said that you can get dressed, surf the web, have a cardio workout, and save the environment all on your drive to work, you might call that person mad. Well, this "insanity" is coming soon to a traffic jam near you.

The impact of stop-and-go traffic on the environment is obvious: wasted fuel, increased CO_2 emissions, global warming. The impact on our psyche is difficult to measure but equally devastating. The lonely commuter spends hours trapped in stop-and-go traffic—semirelaxed yet semivigilant—unable to doze off but also unable to do a thorough job with electric razor or mascara. What he or she yearns for is a trusted driving partner to take over the wheel from time to time.

The following invention brings commuters a helping hand by means of the C.A.N. (Cooperative Automotive Network). When two or more network devices "shake hands," these cars form a "commutal bond" and begin traveling as one. Based on sensors in the lead car, a microchip adjusts the acceleration of the network cars to maintain a safe, sustainable speed—no more stop-and-go driving. Electromagnets hold the network members firmly together to allow data to be shared throughout the chain of vehicles. When the lead car sees a clearing in the traffic ahead, he is free to "unplug" from the C.A.N. and begin traveling alone again. During low-speed networking, the commuter may choose to doze, leave the car for exercise, pursue hobbies, or socialize with fellow commuters.

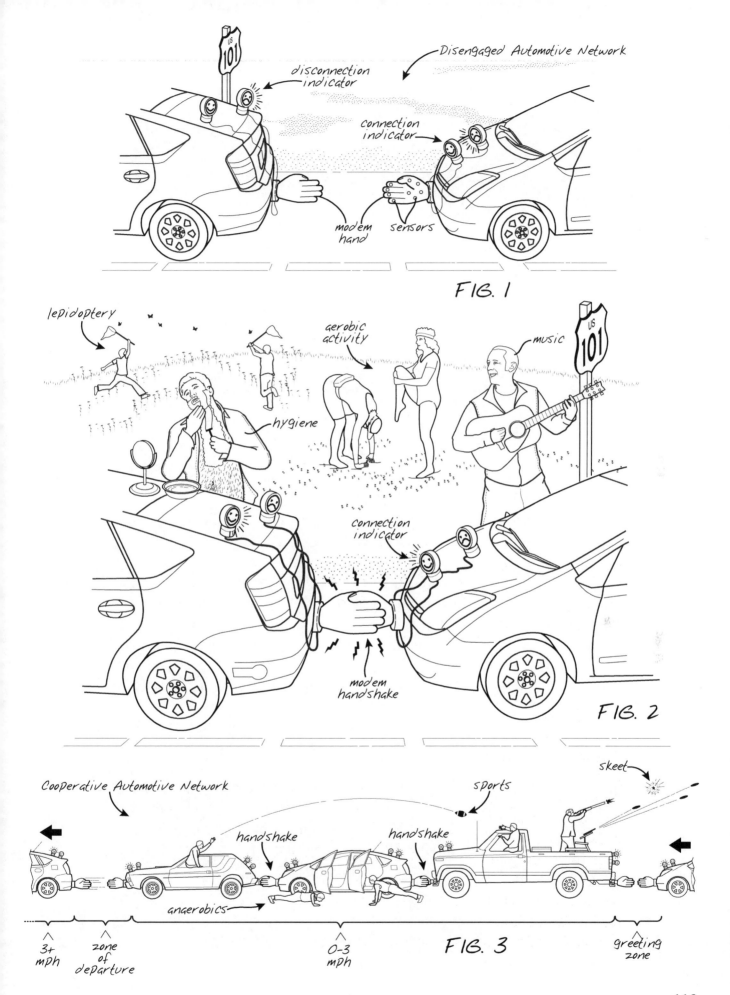

FIG. 1

Disengaged Automotive Network

disconnection indicator

connection indicator

modem hand

sensors

FIG. 2

lepidoptery

aerobic activity

music

hygiene

connection indicator

modem handshake

FIG. 3

Cooperative Automotive Network

sports

skeet

handshake

handshake

anaerobics

3+ mph

zone of departure

0-3 mph

greeting zone

The SMO$_2$GGER

ABSTRACT

A modular, portable emissions purification system for automobiles, utilizing plant life and photosynthetic leafy greens.

BACKGROUND OF INVENTION

Car emissions account for nearly 50 percent of global CO_2 emissions. These gases pass into the atmosphere where they erode holes in the ozone layer. Plants and trees require carbon dioxide (also known as CO_2) for photosynthesis, a process whereby deadly CO_2 gas is converted into clean, life-affirming oxygen (also known as O_2). It has been well documented that plant life thrives when an abundance of CO_2 is present. Unfortunately, most of the automobile emissions drift upwardly to the ozone layer without ever contacting the leaves of plant life for conversion into O_2.

It is a primary objective of the present invention to provide a method and apparatus in which CO_2 emissions from automotive exhaust pipes can be collected and housed in a plant-filled terrarium trailer to allow sufficient time for gas conversion. The modular design allows users to sufficiently outfit a vehicle for Carbonically Neutralized Emissions.

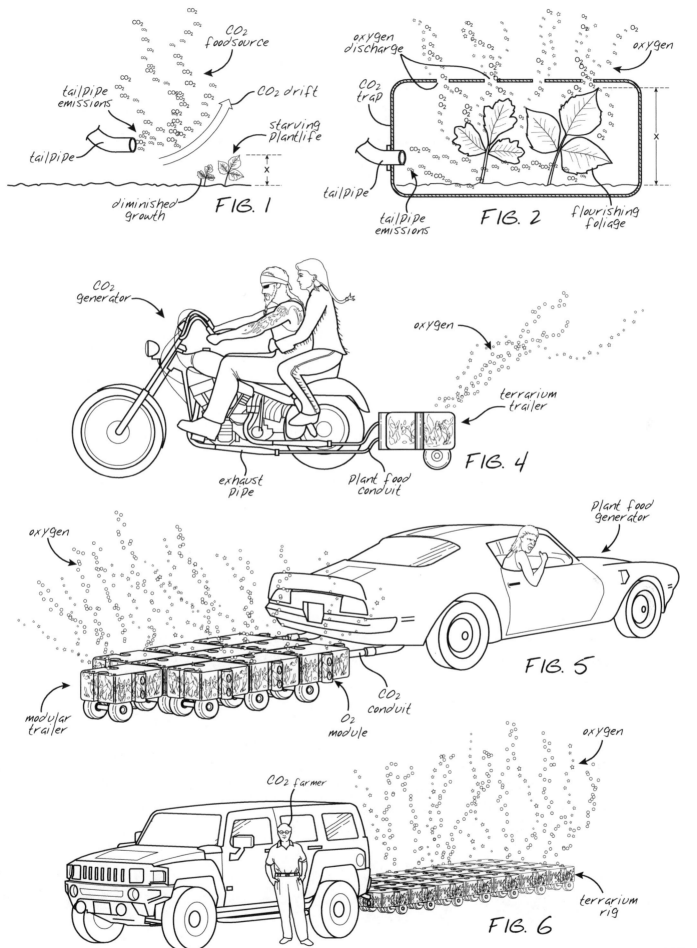

FIG. 1

CO_2 foodsource

tailpipe emissions

tailpipe

CO_2 drift

starving plantlife

X

diminished growth

FIG. 2

oxygen discharge

oxygen

CO_2 trap

tailpipe

tailpipe emissions

X

flourishing foliage

FIG. 4

CO_2 generator

oxygen

terrarium trailer

exhaust pipe

Plant food conduit

FIG. 5

Plant food generator

oxygen

modular trailer

O_2 module

CO_2 conduit

FIG. 6

CO_2 farmer

oxygen

terrarium rig

Global Unwarming StratosFan

ABSTRACT
A colossal exhaust fan that sucks heat and emissions from the earth's atmosphere.

BACKGROUND OF INVENTION
Anyone who has spent time in a windowless bathroom knows the importance of an exhaust fan for removing vapors. The physics of the fan are quite simple: bad air is sucked from the room and blown outdoors, where its lower concentration becomes inoffensive to human senses. Now imagine that the atmospheric bubble surrounding our planet is the "bathroom," with door tightly closed and duct taped. The bad air and humidity rise and accumulate each time the "bathroom" is used, until you finally asphyxiate.

The current invention offers a simple solution to global warming and rising greenhouse gases. An atmospheric exhaust fan, assembled in orbit or launched *in toto*, hovers between the earth's atmosphere and deep space. With the flip of a switch, the earth's atmosphere quickly becomes cooler, cleaner, and more conducive to life. Solar and lunar panels provide a continuous power supply.

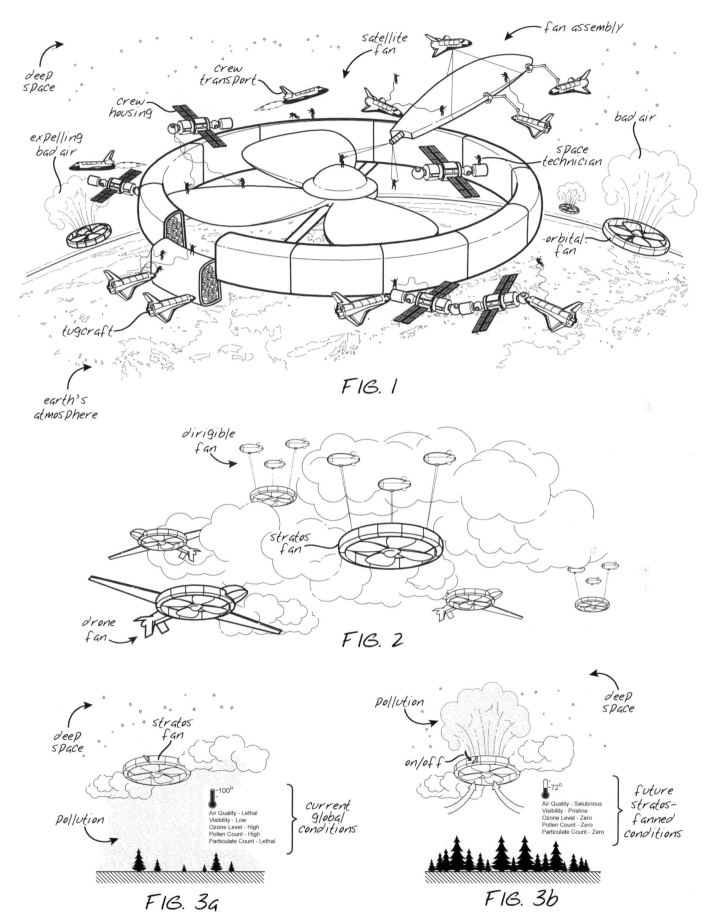

FIG. 1

deep space

expelling bad air

crew housing

crew transport

satellite fan

fan assembly

space technician

bad air

orbital fan

tugcraft

earth's atmosphere

FIG. 2

dirigible fan

stratos fan

drone fan

FIG. 3a

deep space

stratos fan

Pollution

-100°

Air Quality - Lethal
Visibility - Low
Ozone Level - High
Pollen Count - High
Particulate Count - Lethal

current global conditions

FIG. 3b

Pollution

deep space

on/off

-72°

Air Quality - Salubrious
Visibility - Pristine
Ozone Level - Zero
Pollen Count - Zero
Particulate Count - Zero

future stratos-fanned conditions

Chapter VIII.
Frenetics

The high-octane energy output of children and animals is nearly continuous during waking hours. After a nap and a quick snack or grazing, they are refueled and ready to recommence. By gently harnessing these creatures' spirited tendencies, we can establish a fairly clean, perfectly symbiotic energy source.

Children and animals truly are our future.

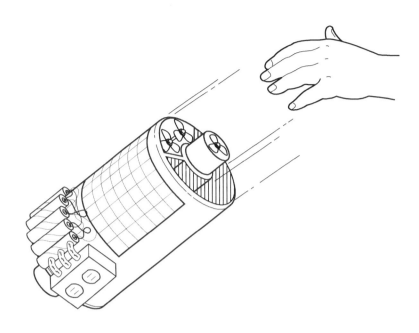

Voltsam And Jetsam

ABSTRACT

A seaborne, wind-driven, plankto-electric-generation vessel.

BACKGROUND OF INVENTION

Since the 1970s, we've been trying to teach our children well. We ask them to respect Mother Earth. We ask them to reduce, reuse, recycle. And, above all, we ask them not to litter. But our children seem hardwired to throw sticks, rocks, and garbage into every body of water they encounter.

The current invention puts this uncontrollable urge to work for us. The alternative energy canister described herein is thrown into a body of water by a child. As it drifts to shore, clean alternative energy is generated. Fortunately, children are equally hardwired to gather debris from the water's edge and will happily amass piles of these canisters at the shoreline. The canisters can then be collected by an adult who will upload the electricity to the grid. The process is hereby complete, and the child will never even know he was unwittingly saving our planet.

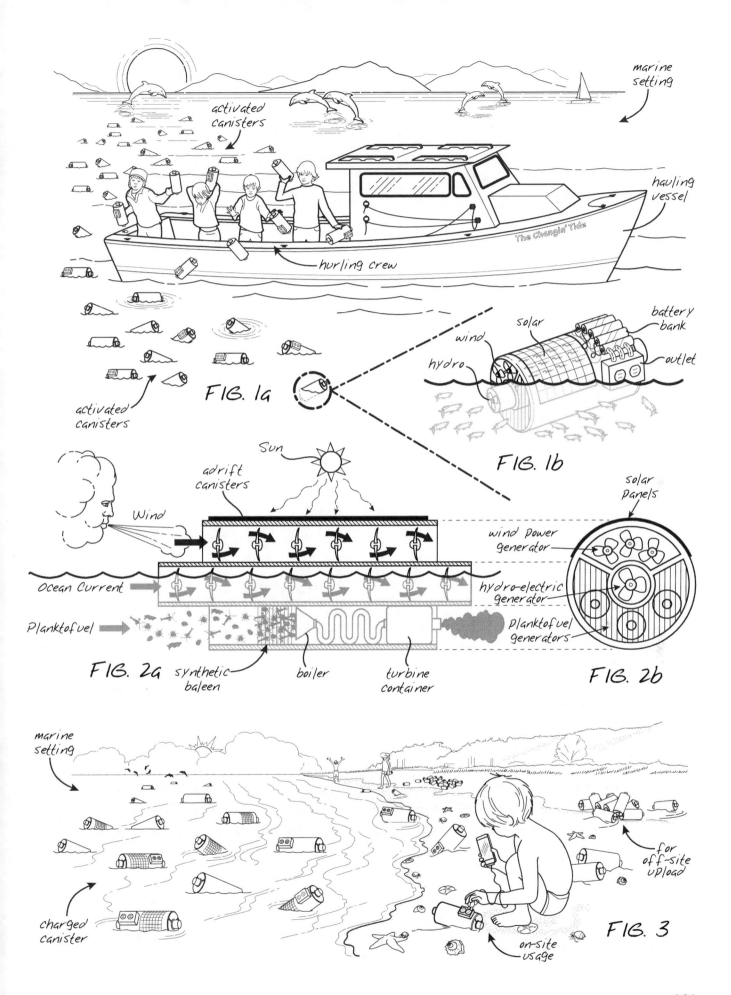

marine setting

activated canisters

hauling vessel

hurling crew

The Changin' Tide

activated canisters

FIG. 1a

wind
solar
hydro
battery bank
outlet

FIG. 1b

Sun

adrift canisters

Wind

Ocean Current

Planktofuel

FIG. 2a   synthetic baleen   boiler   turbine container

solar panels

wind power generator

hydro-electric generator

planktofuel generators

FIG. 2b

marine setting

charged canister

for off-site upload

on-site usage

FIG. 3

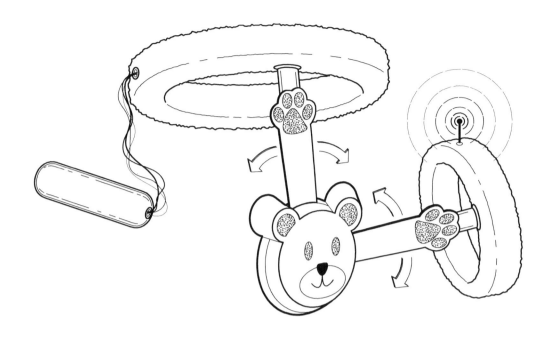

KidNetics

ABSTRACT

An apparatus for harnessing the energy expended by babies, toddlers, and other frenetic diminutives.

BACKGROUND OF INVENTION

The movements of babies and toddlers are a wonderful source of amusement. But with energy output unmatched in the entire animal kingdom, human offspring can offer something much more valuable than mere entertainment: an endless stream of clean, high-yield, harnessable energy. In the past, harnessing such energy was impossible without impeding the child's movements and calling ethics into question.

The invention disclosed herein accomplishes the feat through its use of ultraefficient electrofrictional generators, much like the hand-cranked generators found in emergency radios. These electrical generators are housed within adorable devices in which the generated electricity can be transmitted to holding cells for later use. Plush appendage cuffs offer unmatched comfort for the child.

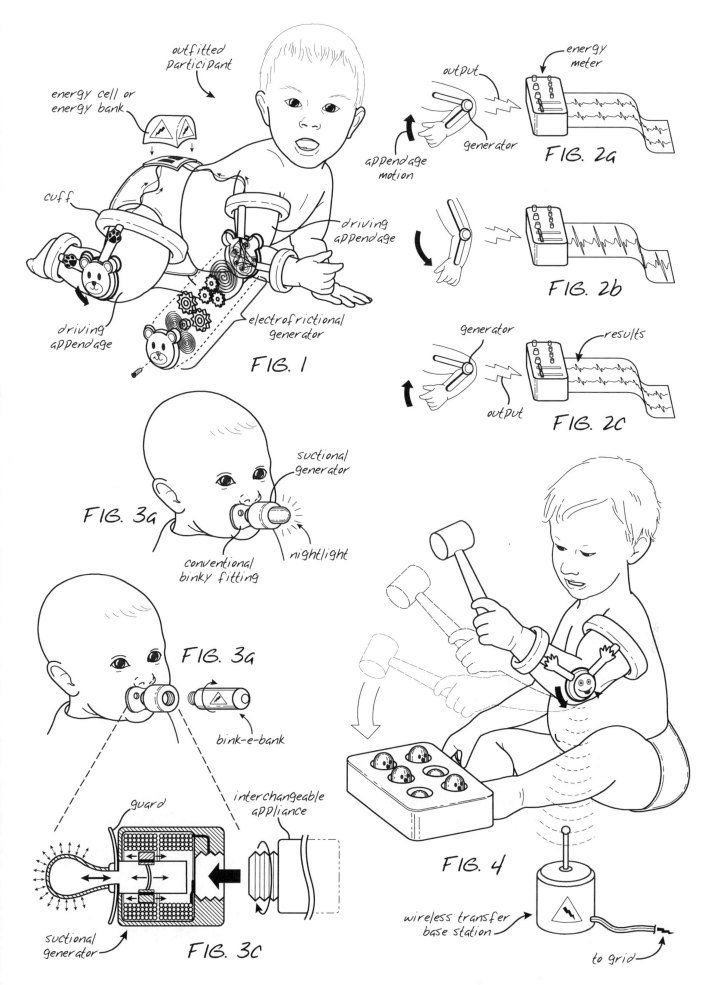

outfitted Participant

energy cell or energy bank

cuff

driving appendage

driving appendage

electrofrictional generator

FIG. 1

output

appendage motion

generator

energy meter

FIG. 2a

FIG. 2b

generator

results

output

FIG. 2c

FIG. 3a

suctional generator

conventional binky fitting

nightlight

FIG. 3a

bink-e-bank

guard

interchangeable appliance

suctional generator

FIG. 3c

FIG. 4

wireless transfer base station

to grid

Energy Trap

ABSTRACT

A deep pitfall lined with conveyer-type rollers that convert the frantic movements of an entrapped wild beast into clean, renewable electricity.

BACKGROUND OF INVENTION

Tribal peoples around the world are no longer content with ancient pastimes and traditions. Activities that appealed to their forefathers pale in comparison to the exciting and addictive activities of the West. They now demand our modern entertainment and conveniences, and they require the electricity it takes to run them. In order to meet this demand, we need to develop alternative energy sources that employ local resources.

The current invention will supply limitless wattage to underdeveloped areas by humanely exploiting local wildlife. The "manpower" for these devices will be provided by medium-to-large animals that stumble into the pitfall. As the beasts scramble to escape the trap, they drive roller-style electrical generators. The animals also benefit from this high-intensity, low-impact aerobic workout.

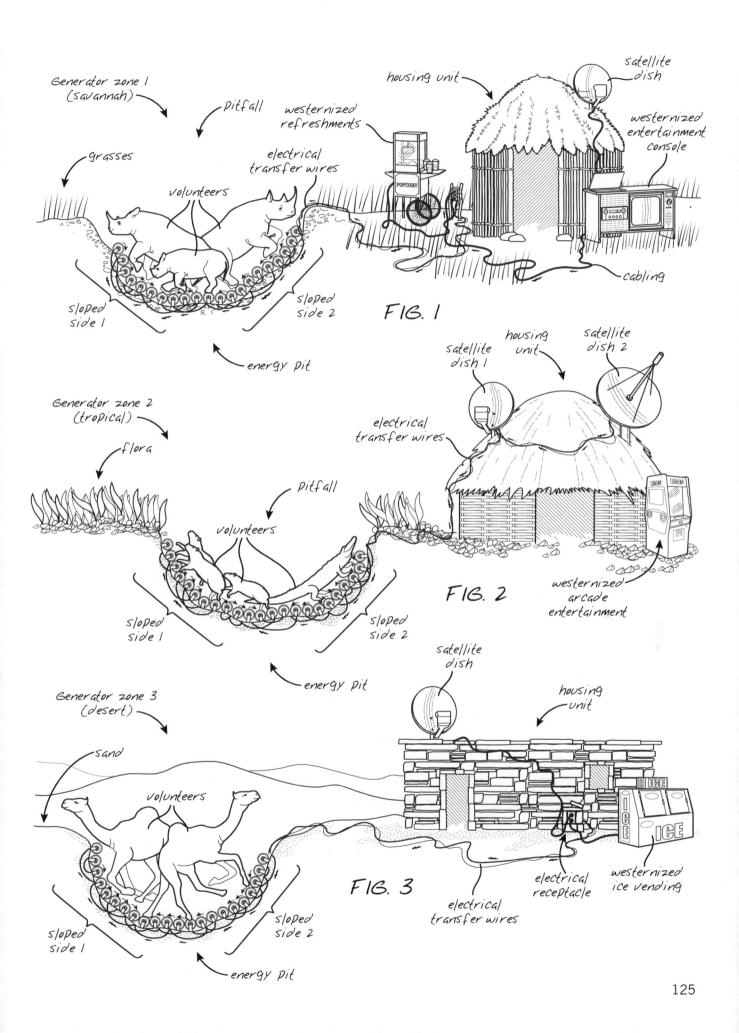

Generator zone 1 (savannah)

grasses

Pitfall

westernized refreshments

electrical transfer wires

volunteers

housing unit

satellite dish

westernized entertainment console

sloped side 1

sloped side 2

energy pit

POPCORN

cabling

FIG. 1

Generator zone 2 (tropical)

flora

Pitfall

volunteers

sloped side 1

sloped side 2

energy pit

satellite dish 1

housing unit

satellite dish 2

electrical transfer wires

westernized arcade entertainment

FIG. 2

Generator zone 3 (desert)

sand

volunteers

satellite dish

housing unit

sloped side 1

sloped side 2

energy pit

electrical receptacle

electrical transfer wires

westernized ice vending

ICE

FIG. 3

125

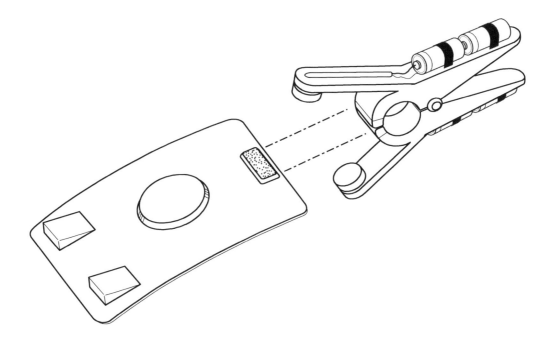

Spokenergy

ABSTRACT

A microflap flip electrical generator for insertion between the spokes of a tricycle or other wheeled vehicle.

BACKGROUND OF INVENTION

A bicycle wheel travels around its axel just one time per pedal rotation. So during an average bike ride of 5,000 pedal rotations, a traditional pedal-powered electrical generator experiences just 5,000 ECMs, or Electrically Chargeable Moments. By contrast, 48 spokes travel around the axel during that same pedaling sequence, nearly 250,000 times per bike ride. And each time one of these 48 spokes passes the wheel's fork or frame we are presented with Electrically Chargeable Moments to be seized or lost forever.

The invention disclosed herein employs a flipping microflap spring generator mounted on a bicycle to convert spoke strikes into clean, sustainable electricity. An optional muffling cover allows for stealth riding.

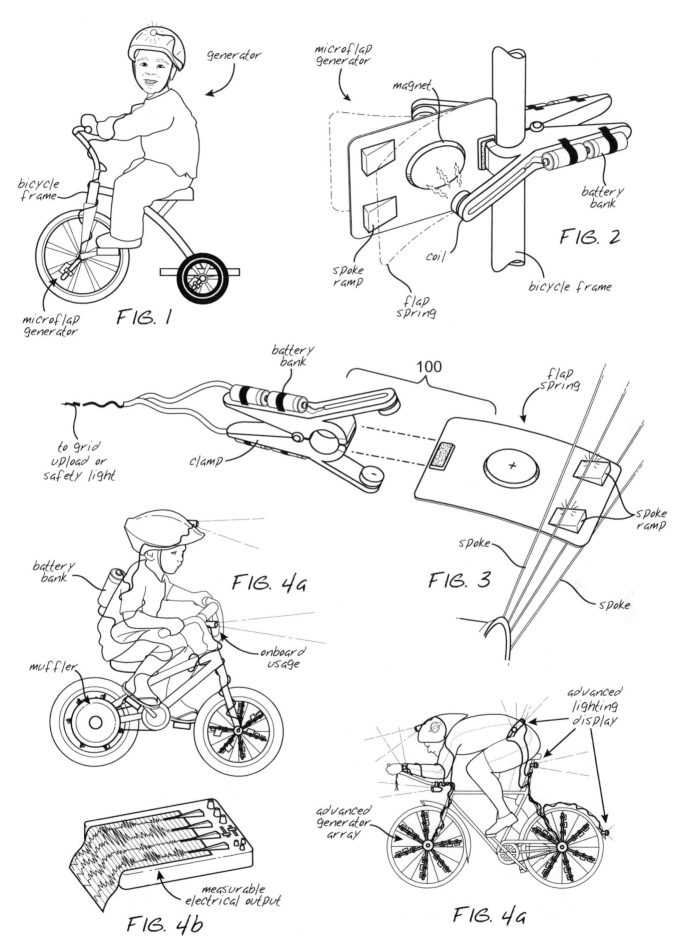

generator

microflap
generator

bicycle
frame

microflap
generator

FIG. 1

magnet

spoke
ramp

coil

flap
spring

battery
bank

bicycle frame

FIG. 2

battery
bank

100

flap
spring

to grid
upload or
safety light

clamp

spoke

spoke
ramp

spoke

FIG. 3

battery
bank

FIG. 4a

muffler

onboard
usage

advanced
lighting
display

advanced
generator
array

measurable
electrical output

FIG. 4b

FIG. 4a

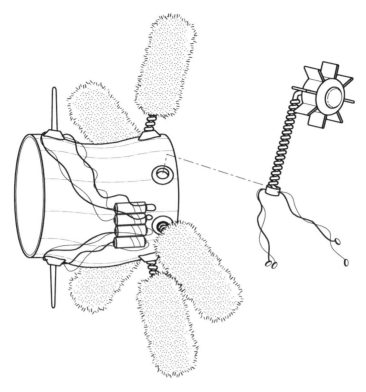

Canine Agilitricity

ABSTRACT

A girdle for canines that generates and captures electricity during agility training and shows.

BACKGROUND OF INVENTION

Anyone who has attended a dog show knows the thrill of watching canines maneuver around the agility course. Through hoops, tunnels, and weave poles, the dogs navigate the obstacles with jaw-dropping precision. And now, science is making this astonishing event absolutely electrifying.

For the one to two minutes that a typical dog races around an agility course, the animal is in continual contact with the obstacles. As he glides past the surfaces of the obstacles, enormous amounts of static electricity build in the canine's fur. Sadly, the charges are depleted by the time the animal reaches the finish line.

The current invention offers a means of capturing and storing this static electricity. Fitted with a nonlethal "lightning rod" and lightweight battery pack, the canines will unwittingly generate clean energy as they race through the course. Fuzzy, conductive materials can be affixed to the show animal to increase static electricity. The stored electricity can be used on demand at the show or uploaded to the grid. At the event's conclusion, electricity that is generated by each dog can be measured, with bonus points awarded for wattage production.

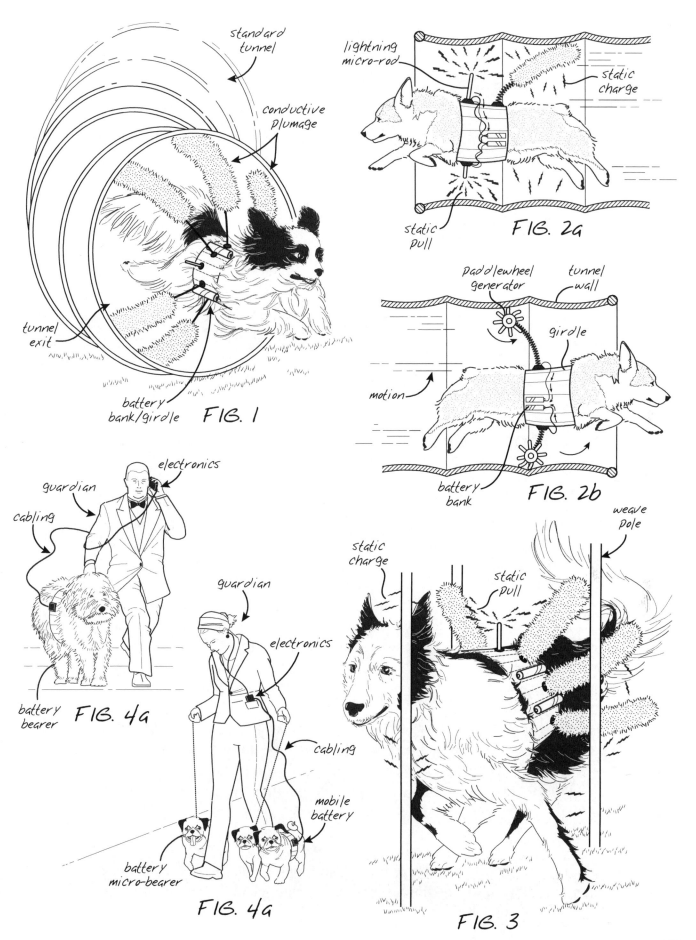

standard
tunnel

conductive
plumage

tunnel
exit

battery
bank/girdle

FIG. 1

lightning
micro-rod

static
charge

static
pull

FIG. 2a

paddlewheel
generator

tunnel
wall

girdle

motion

battery
bank

FIG. 2b

electronics

guardian

cabling

battery
bearer

FIG. 4a

guardian

electronics

cabling

mobile
battery

battery
micro-bearer

FIG. 4a

static
charge

static
pull

weave
pole

FIG. 3

Catnap Inertia Trap

ABSTRACT

An exceedingly comfortable bedding platform that uses the weight of a cat's resting body to drive or recharge pampering devices for the animal.

BACKGROUND OF INVENTION

Pet guardians have been pampering their felines with battery-operated paraphernalia since 1971, when the first battery-powered cat toy was invented. As the market became flooded with these devices, pet guardians blithely embraced battery power as a cheap and disposable means of coddling one's pets. But recent scientific data shows trace amounts of battery toxins appearing in municipal tap water: the same water we serve to our cats. Now, the pet guardian is faced with a conundrum: should he continue to buy these battery-powered products and risk poisoning his cats, or should he curb the poisoning and risk damaging his loving relationship with his cats?

The current invention solves the problem. The system includes a luxurious bedding platform, a central pole around which the platform spirals downward, a gear train, and a windup spring unit. The pole might additionally be housed in a familiar exterior, like a tree, a curtain, or a human leg, to encourage the animal to climb and roost on the platform.

With this device, your sleeping cat becomes the driving force behind a windup mechanism, thereby providing sufficient power for its own needs. A plug-and-play interface allows several kitty stations to be run simultaneously from a single nap windup.

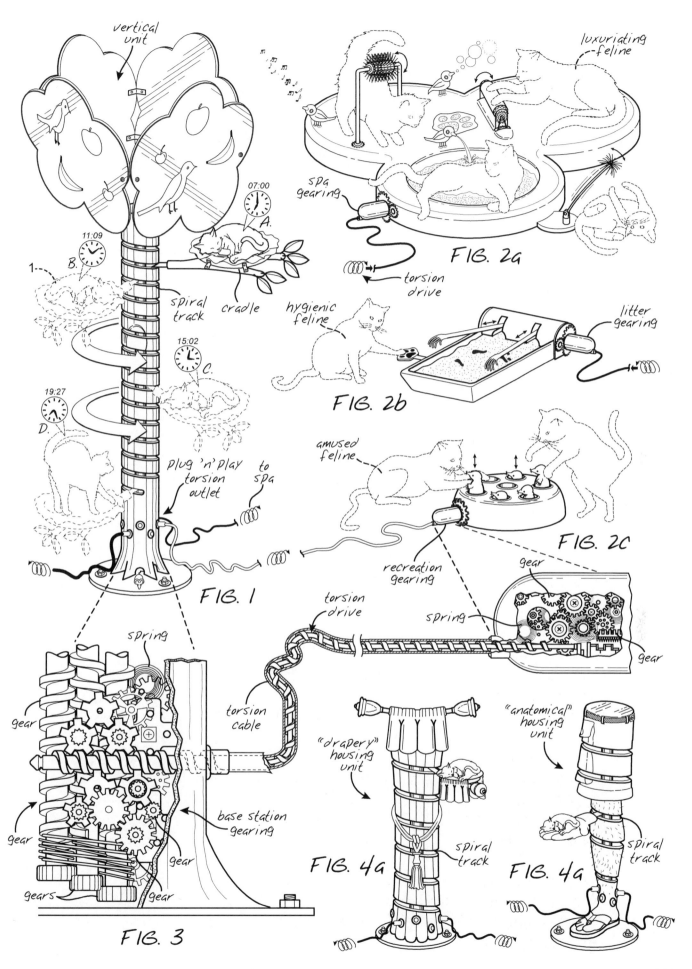

vertical unit

07:00
A.

11:09
B.

1

15:02
C.

19:27
D.

spiral track

cradle

plug 'n' play torsion outlet

to spa

FIG. 1

luxuriating feline

spa gearing

torsion drive

FIG. 2a

hygienic feline

litter gearing

FIG. 2b

amused feline

recreation gearing

gear

spring

gear

FIG. 2c

spring

gear

gear

gear

gears

gear

torsion cable

base station gearing

FIG. 3

torsion drive

"drapery" housing unit

spiral track

FIG. 4a

"anatomical" housing unit

spiral track

FIG. 4a

Chapter IX.
Alternative Energy Alternatives

I started listening to alternative music as a teenager. Soon
after, everyone began listening to my music—alternative
became mainstream. The same is true with alternative
energy: everyone is doing solar, wind, and geothermal.

It's time to rethink alternative and see if we can find its alternative.

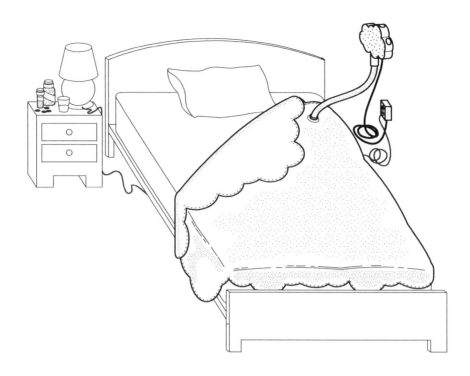

EZ-Z-Z-Z Electrical Generator

ABSTRACT

A system for capturing heat that is radiated and expelled by sleeping bodies, for use in the generation of electricity.

BACKGROUND OF INVENTION

The present invention is based on the principals set forth in the dry-steam power plant design of 1896. In that model, geothermal heat was used to drive turbine blades of an electrical generator. In the current invention, however, geothermal energy has been substituted with Triothermal™ energy: *body heat*, *respiratory humidity,* and *flatus*. Since the amount of electricity that these generators can produce is directly controlled by the output of the three heat sources, there is particular benefit to increasing the thermal output and subduvet temperature. The use of nonporous fabrics, such as plastic, in the bed environment has been shown in studies to significantly increase body temperatures. In addition, the consumption of concentrated legume supplements, like Wind-EZ™, can increase the thermal intensiveness of gas expulsion.

The components of this system include a modified duvet comforter and/or respiratory umbrella, convection-powered electrical generator, connective hoses, and an electrical transformer with a receptacle for powering small bedroom appliances.

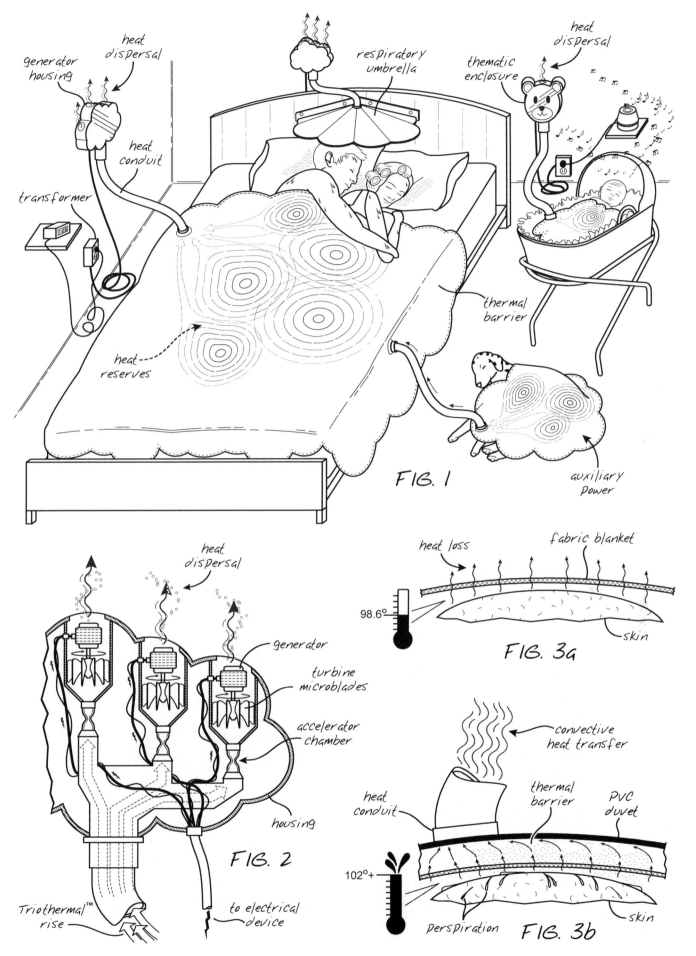

FIG. 1

generator housing

heat dispersal

heat conduit

transformer

heat reserves

respiratory umbrella

thermal barrier

heat dispersal

thematic enclosure

auxiliary power

FIG. 2

heat dispersal

generator

turbine microblades

accelerator chamber

housing

Triothermal™ rise

to electrical device

FIG. 3a

heat loss

fabric blanket

98.6°

skin

FIG. 3b

convective heat transfer

heat conduit

thermal barrier

PVC duvet

102°+

perspiration

skin

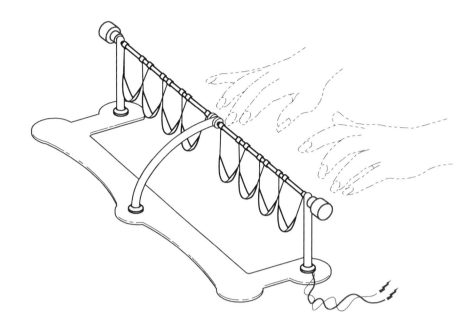

Digit Hammock

ABSTRACT

An electrical generator that uses a standard pulley/hammock system to convert the movement of one's digits into electrical current.

BACKGROUND OF INVENTION

Imagine the following ad in your local newspaper: *Help Wanted: Experienced secretary with energetic personality and muscular hands. Minimum typing speed of 60 microwatts per minute*. Within years this ad will be a reality.

As far back as the industrial revolution, scientists have used treadmills fitted with coils and magnets to generate small electrical currents. In the 1960s and '70s, when our country was heady with the Fitness Craze, many U.S. companies developed portable electrical generators. When fastened to the legs and/or feet of an individual, these devices could generate significant electricity during exercise. Many Americans viewed this moment as the new dawn of clean electricity. But with the growth of personal computing in the 1990s, people began sitting more and walking less. Today, many of America's workers spend 100 percent of their workday in front of personal computers. According to one study, many office workers travel farther with their fingers across keyboards and smart phones than they travel with their legs to and from the office. Isn't it time to let your fingers do the walking to a clean energy future?

The current invention employs generators, geared like hand-crank radios, to capture the motion of keystrokes and finger gestures. These nanoelectrical generators can be modified for use in other digit-intensive activities.

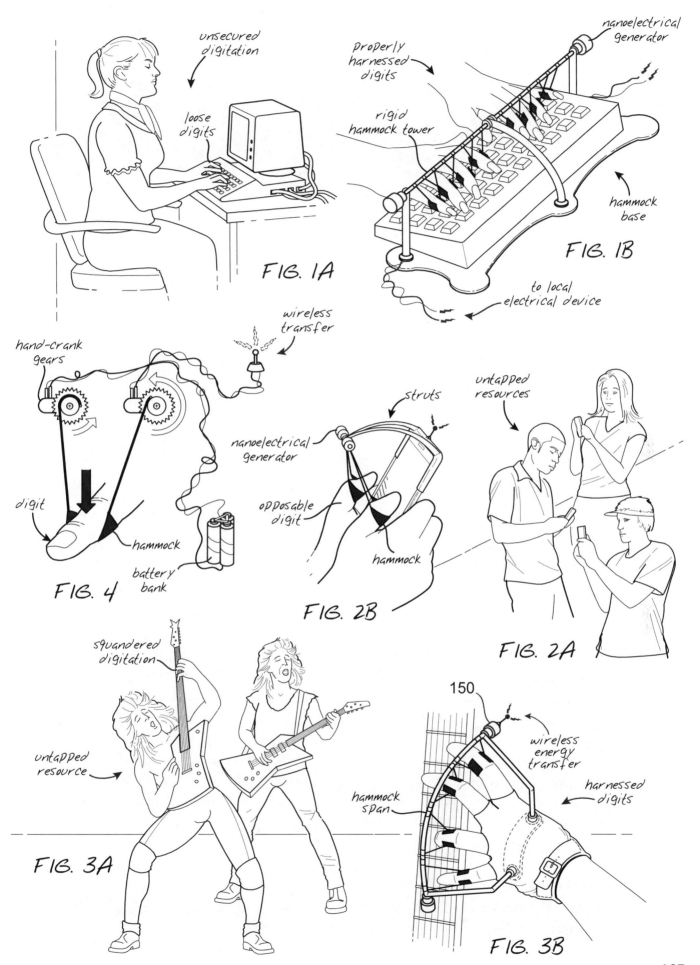

unsecured digitation

loose digits

FIG. 1A

properly harnessed digits

rigid hammock tower

nanoelectrical generator

hammock base

FIG. 1B

to local electrical device

wireless transfer

hand-crank gears

digit

hammock

battery bank

FIG. 4

nanoelectrical generator

opposable digit

struts

hammock

FIG. 2B

untapped resources

FIG. 2A

squandered digitation

untapped resource

FIG. 3A

150

wireless energy transfer

harnessed digits

hammock span

FIG. 3B

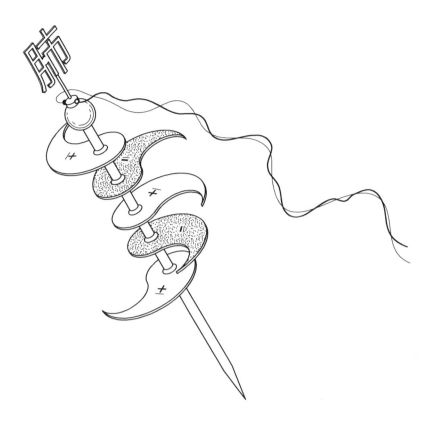

Chi Mill

ABSTRACT

An acupuncture needle comprising yin and/or yang blades and a nanoelectrical generator. Networks of needles clustered along central meridians can generate adequate electrical output to supply current for moxibustion therapy or handheld appliances.

BACKGROUND OF INVENTION

Ancient teachings have described the force of chi as *the mighty river, the monsoon, the mouse*. Disregarding the "*mouse*" comparison, one can appreciate the enormous potential of this vital energy force. Standard filiform needles have been used for eons to reestablish chi flow in the body through the manipulation and reduction of blockages in meridians. In traditional acupuncture, a small but not insignificant amount of chi, known as "energy updraft," is released at the insertion site. The radiant chi spews upward and quickly dissipates into the cosmic energy flow. Unlike traditional needles, the current invention captures this valuable "updraft" with its turbine blades. The resulting pinwheel effect drives the nanoelectrical generator, creating renewable *chi-lectricity*.

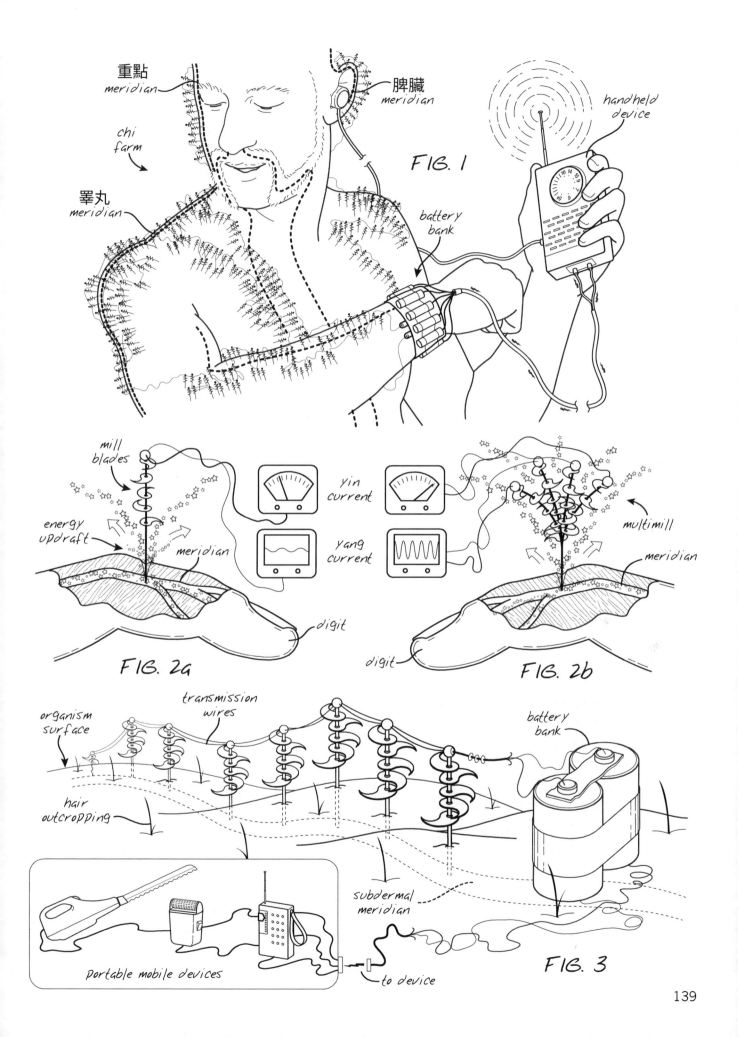

重點
meridian

脾臟
meridian

chi farm

睪丸
meridian

FIG. 1

handheld device

battery bank

mill blades

energy updraft

meridian

yin current

yang current

digit

FIG. 2a

multimill

meridian

digit

FIG. 2b

organism surface

transmission wires

battery bank

hair outcropping

subdermal meridian

Portable mobile devices

to device

FIG. 3

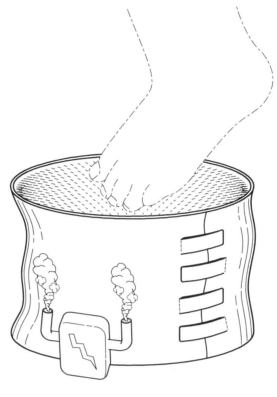

Cellul-i-tricity

ABSTRACT

An elastomeric band with a plurality of pain-free hypodermic needles that siphon fat from human hypodermis for fueling an electrical microgenerator.

BACKGROUND OF INVENTION

What would losing 20 pounds mean to *you*? Maybe it means dropping one or two dress sizes. Or finally fitting into your prom tuxedo after all these years. In the near future, losing 20 pounds will mean free electricity via the most renewable fuel source known to man: clean-burning, nontoxic, organic human fat.

Unlike mainstream fuel sources that lie deep underground, fields of energy-rich fat lie a mere centimeter below the skin's surface—no deep-sea drilling or costly exploration required. There is also no need for expensive transportation charges getting the fuel to market; the electrical generator is housed *on site*! The hypodermic needles lack moving parts, so they will never break down like traditional drilling rigs. And with hundreds of microscopic needles accessing the field simultaneously, the reserves are mined slowly and evenly without leaving a pocked surface from depleted resources below the skin. Optionally, the lipo-rig can be outfitted with warming and/or agitation devices to loosen the subcutaneous reservoirs before mining.

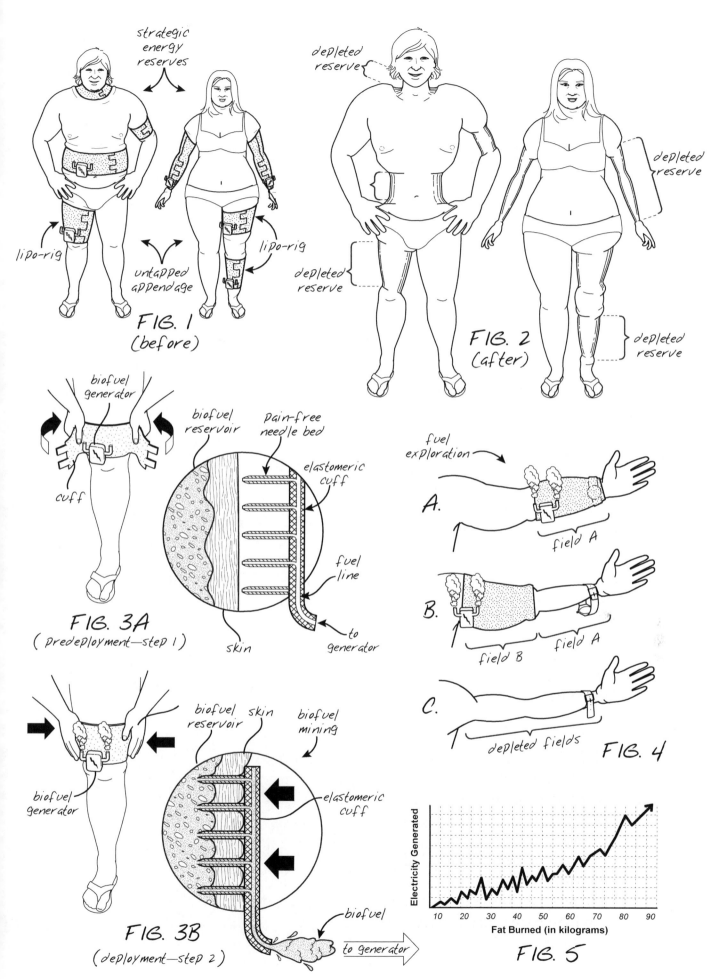

FIG. 1
(before)

strategic energy reserves

lipo-rig

untapped appendage

FIG. 2
(after)

depleted reserve

depleted reserve

depleted reserve

biofuel generator

cuff

FIG. 3A
(predeployment—step 1)

biofuel reservoir

pain-free needle bed

elastomeric cuff

fuel line

to generator

skin

fuel exploration

A.

field A

B.

field B   field A

C.

depleted fields

FIG. 4

biofuel generator

biofuel reservoir

skin

biofuel mining

elastomeric cuff

biofuel

to generator

FIG. 3B
(deployment—step 2)

Electricity Generated

Fat Burned (in kilograms)

10 20 30 40 50 60 70 80 90

FIG. 5

141

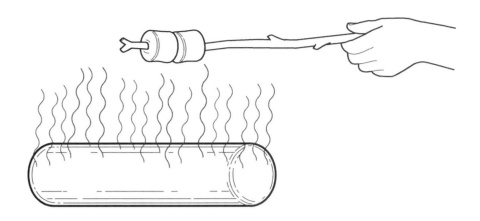

HotRods

ABSTRACT

A rod used to transfer heat from a car engine into a home.

BACKGROUND OF INVENTION

If you could reduce global warming during your Sunday drive, wouldn't you take that drive every day of the week?

We're all concerned about rising global temperatures. We want to help cool Mother Earth, but we just don't know where to start. New research indicates that each of us can make an impact on global temperatures by simply reducing our reliance on the top three domestic heat sources: our ovens, our furnaces, and our cars. Now, obviously we can't live without our cars. So, how can we reduce our cooking and our heating without also starving and freezing?

The current invention reclaims the heat from our car engines and reuses it in our homes. Heat absorption rods made of metal, carbonite, or silica (the lightweight material used in space shuttle tiles) are placed around the engine compartment of an automobile. After the engine has been running and the rods have trapped sufficient heat, these rods can be transported into the home and put to use. The rods can be decorated to resemble wooden logs or branches to add rustic charm to your indoor heating event.

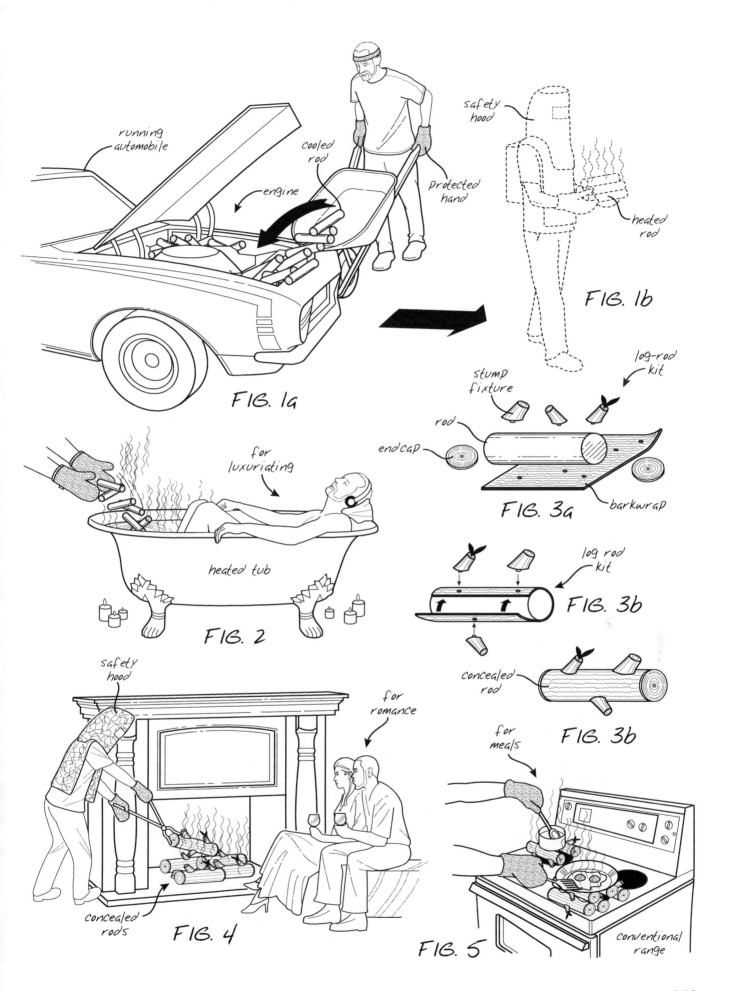

running automobile

cooled rod

engine

protected hand

FIG. 1a

safety hood

heated rod

FIG. 1b

for luxuriating

heated tub

FIG. 2

stump fixture

log-rod kit

rod

endcap

barkwrap

FIG. 3a

log rod kit

FIG. 3b

concealed rod

FIG. 3b

safety hood

for romance

concealed rods

FIG. 4

for meals

conventional range

FIG. 5

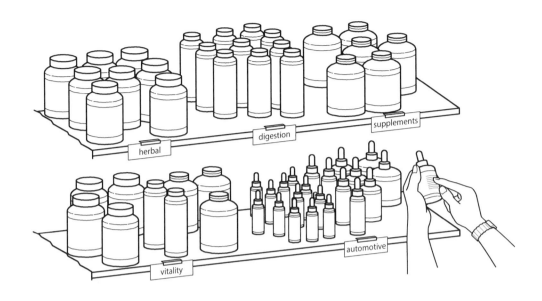

Homeopatholine

ABSTRACT

A method for producing high-performance, depetroleumized homeopathic gasoline for use in small engines.

BACKGROUND OF INVENTION

Since 1755, when Christian Hahnemann introduced homeopathy to the world, scientists have been producing stronger medicines through weaker dilutions. The well-founded laws of homeopathy teach that the true power potency of a given substance is released only after successive shaking and dilution. Sort of like nuclear fission, the small essential particles of a substance must be agitated in order to release their true power potential. As the substance becomes more active and vigorous through subsequent agitation, an infinitesimal amount of the substance is needed to achieve the desired effect. The present invention offers methods for diluting gasoline into robust fuel through ritualistic agitation.

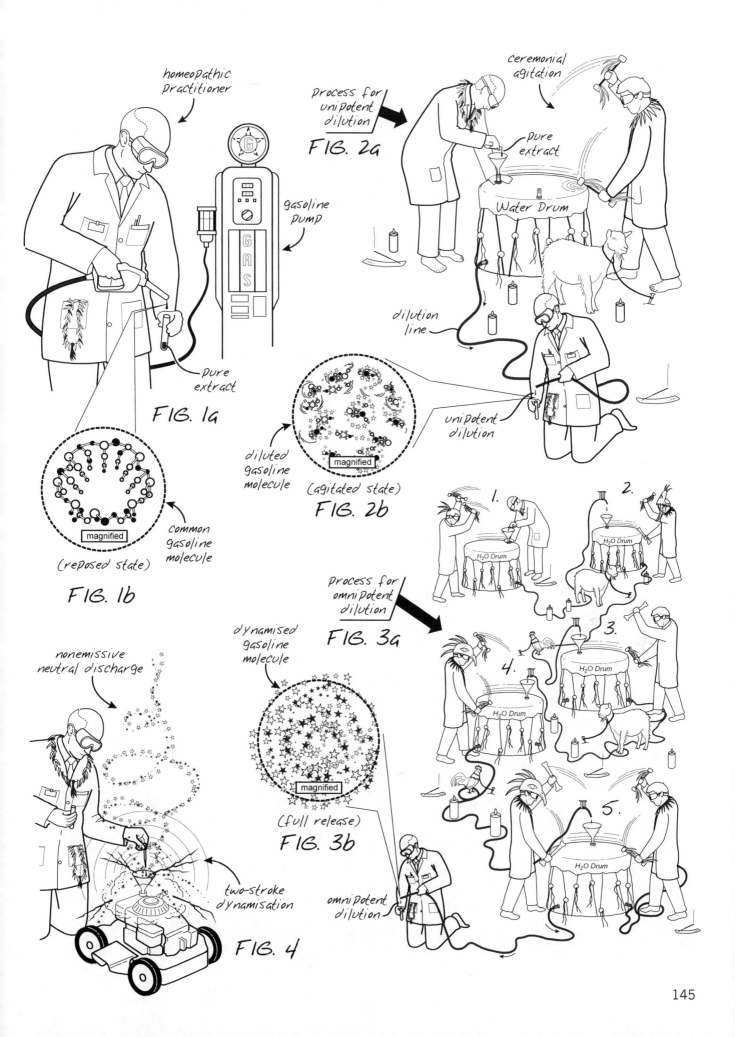

homeopathic practitioner

gasoline pump

pure extract

FIG. 1a

magnified

(reposed state)

FIG. 1b

common gasoline molecule

nonemissive neutral discharge

two-stroke dynamisation

FIG. 4

dynamised gasoline molecule

magnified

(full release)

FIG. 3b

omnipotent dilution

Process for unipotent dilution

FIG. 2a

ceremonial agitation

pure extract

Water Drum

dilution line

unipotent dilution

diluted gasoline molecule

magnified

(agitated state)

FIG. 2b

Process for omnipotent dilution

FIG. 3a

1.

H₂O Drum

2.

H₂O Drum

3.

H₂O Drum

4.

H₂O Drum

5.

H₂O Drum

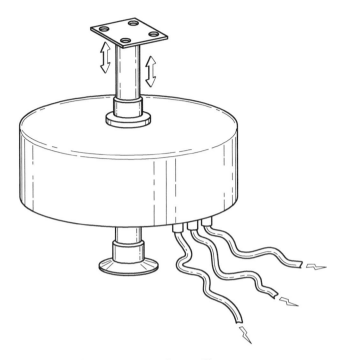

Bounce-Driven Electrical Generator

ABSTRACT

A system for converting the jarring motion of a bus ride into clean electricity for commuters. The essential elements include one electrical generator and one imperfect road surface, formed naturally or engineered.

BACKGROUND OF INVENTION

Bouncing is an unavoidable part of commuting. Whether we are soothed to sleep by gentle vibrations from the road surface or scalded by our lattes during the violent jolt from a pothole, we bounce our way to the office every day. In fact, the combined vertical distance traveled by each bouncing passenger can reach 4,500 feet by trip's end. Amazingly enough, studies have shown that public transit riders, who rank among the most patient and durable members of society, appear completely unfazed when the frequency of potholes is tripled or even quadrupled during laboratory experiments.

The present invention employs a linear-motion electrical generator to harness the vertical motion of bouncing passengers in a bus. The generator would most effectively be mounted under a rider's seat, but the device could also be integrated into handgrips, rails, and floor panels to capture the concussive movements of standing passengers. Road surfaces could be roughened, undulated, or pitted to enhance electrical output. The energy can be stored or used on site to supply commuters with enough electricity to keep them distracted by their electronic devices.

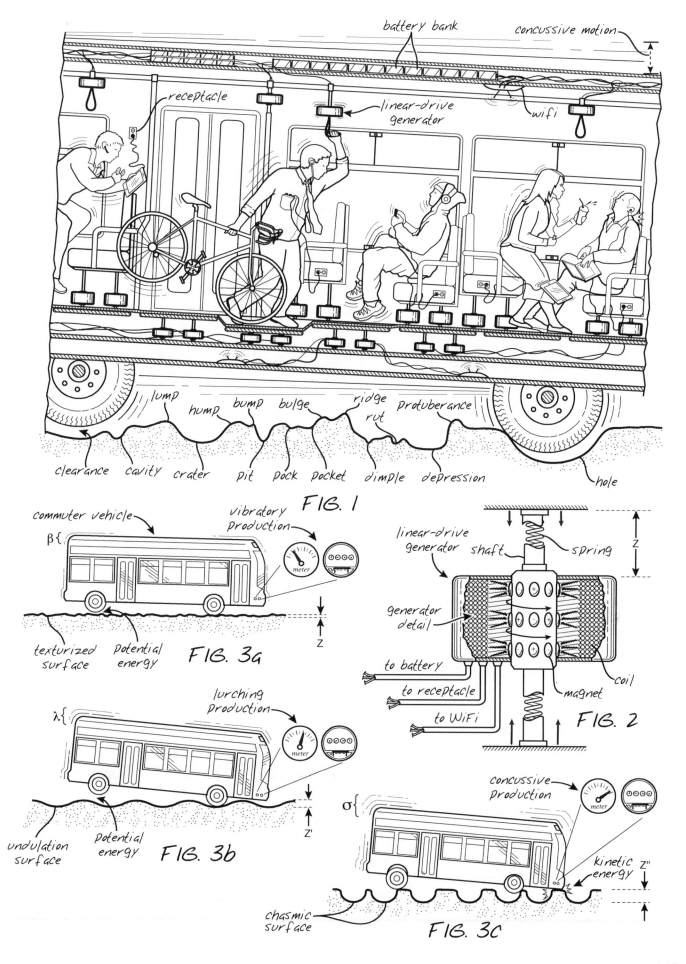

battery bank

concussive motion

receptacle

linear-drive generator

wifi

lump

hump

bump bulge

ridge rut

protuberance

clearance cavity crater pit pock pocket dimple depression hole

FIG. 1

commuter vehicle

β{

vibratory production

meter

texturized surface

potential energy

FIG. 3a

Z

linear-drive generator

shaft spring

Z

generator detail

to battery

to receptacle

to WiFi

coil

magnet

FIG. 2

λ{

lurching production

meter

undulation surface

potential energy

FIG. 3b

Z'

σ{

concussive production

meter

kinetic energy

Z"

chasmic surface

FIG. 3c

Electric Avenue

ABSTRACT

A thoroughfare devoted exclusively to users of alternative energy
and energy conservation.

BACKGROUND OF INVENTION

Dancers have their discotheques. Cowboys have their rodeos. Seniors have
their centers. But where do all of the like-minded, eco-friendly, carbon-
neutral, repurposing citizens of this planet get together?

Electric Avenue.

Each day of your life you try to make the right choices to help save our
planet. Often these small acts are done privately, in the home or at the recycling center, with no one to appreciate you but yourself. Wouldn't it be nice
to have a meeting place where you and others could show the world all the
wonderful things you are doing to save it—a place where people will
acknowledge you for the incredibly great job you are doing? Electric Avenue
is a road set aside exclusively for people who are reducing, reusing, and
reinventing to save Mother Earth. It's sort of like a pedestrian district but
much more exclusive. The location of these avenues will be in high-profile
areas where the message of alternative energy and sustainable transportation
can garner maximum attention.

FIG. 1

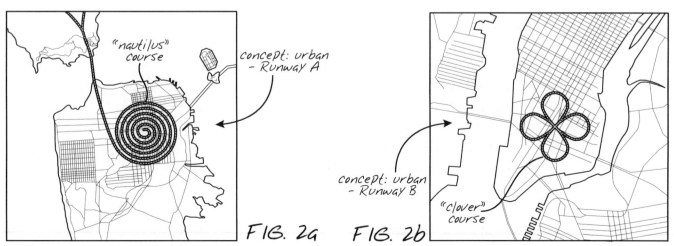

FIG. 2a   FIG. 2b

PART THREE
The Future

Chapter X.
A Future

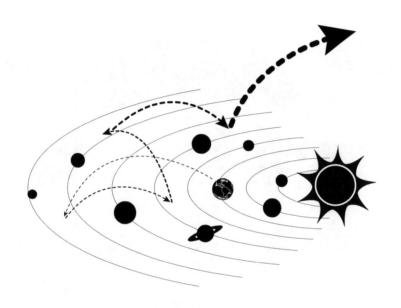

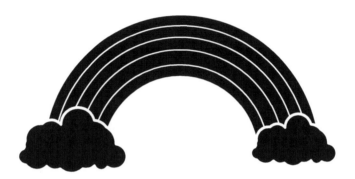

While experts agree that this book has solved most of earth's problems, we mustn't become complacent here on terra firma.

The exciting future of this *unventional* movement lies in the heavens above.

Inventor: Thomas D. W. von Giesler
Title: *An advanced method for collecting highly enriched atmospheric light particles for use in clean, renewable, beautiful energy.*
Filing date: TBD

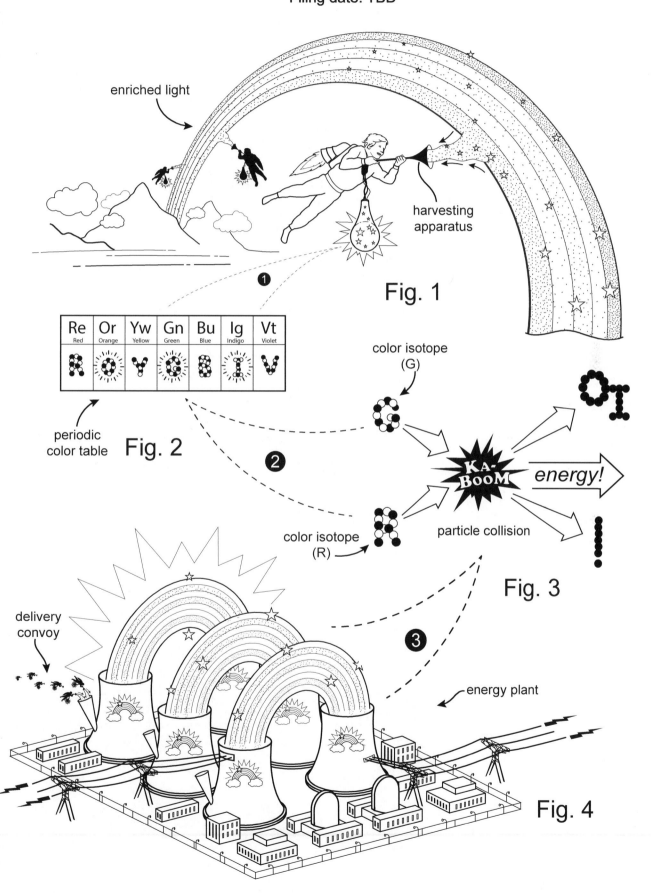

enriched light

harvesting apparatus

Fig. 1

Re	Or	Yw	Gn	Bu	Ig	Vt
Red	Orange	Yellow	Green	Blue	Indigo	Violet

periodic color table

Fig. 2

color isotope (G)

color isotope (R)

KA-BOOM

particle collision

energy!

Fig. 3

delivery convoy

energy plant

Fig. 4

I foresee a day when reserves of water will be conveniently stored in the vast skies just overhead;

Inventor: Thomas D. W. von Giesler
Title: *An advanced method for rustling, wrangling, and/or herding clouds, and device for extracting the same*
Filing date: TBD

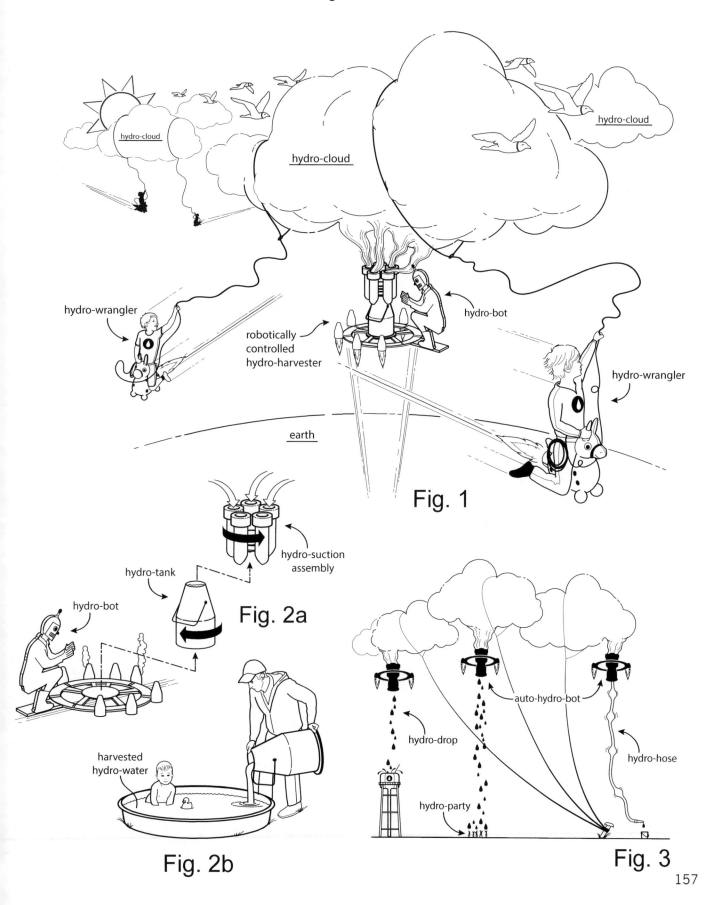

Fig. 1

Fig. 2a

Fig. 2b

Fig. 3

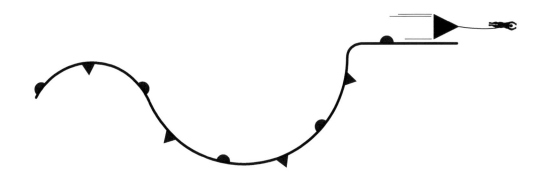

a day when the harsh weather patterns of an angry planet
become docile, malleable, and predictable;

Inventor: Thomas D. W. von Giesler
Title: *An advanced method and system for maintaining, controlling, establishing, and/or reclaiming weather fronts.*
Filing date: TBD

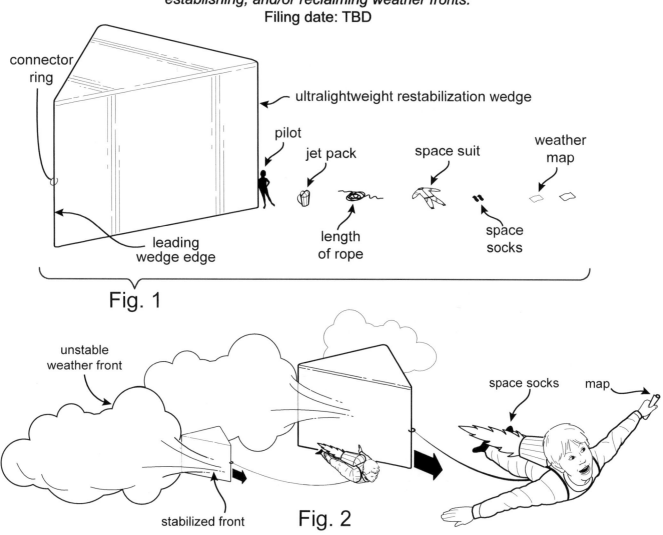

connector ring

ultralightweight restabilization wedge

pilot

jet pack

space suit

weather map

length of rope

space socks

leading wedge edge

Fig. 1

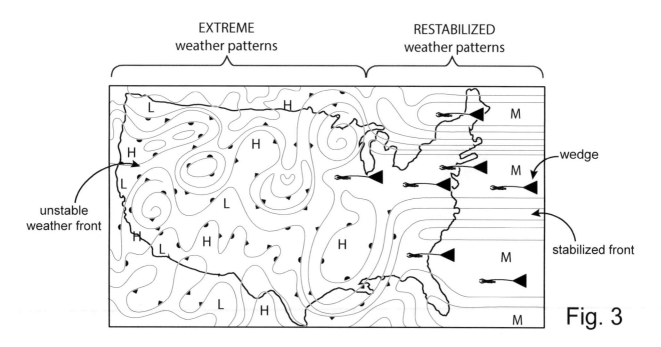

unstable weather front

space socks

map

stabilized front

Fig. 2

EXTREME weather patterns

RESTABILIZED weather patterns

L H H M

H M

wedge

unstable weather front

L L

L

H

L H M

H

stabilized front

L H M

Fig. 3

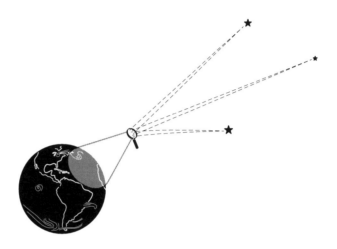

a day when we finally end
our dependence on the sun;

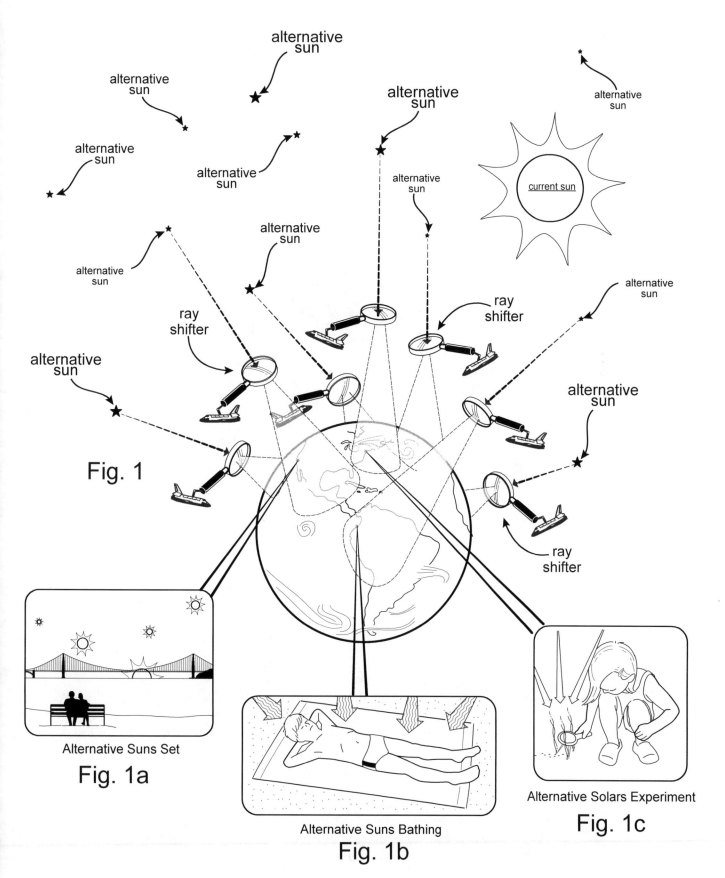

Fig. 1

Alternative Suns Set

Fig. 1a

Alternative Suns Bathing

Fig. 1b

Alternative Solars Experiment

Fig. 1c

and a day when the moon, with its pristine lunar resources,
joins our overcrowded planet for convenient colonization.

Inventor: Thomas D. W. von Giesler
Title: *An advanced method for dismantling and docking celestial bodies.*
Filing date: TBD

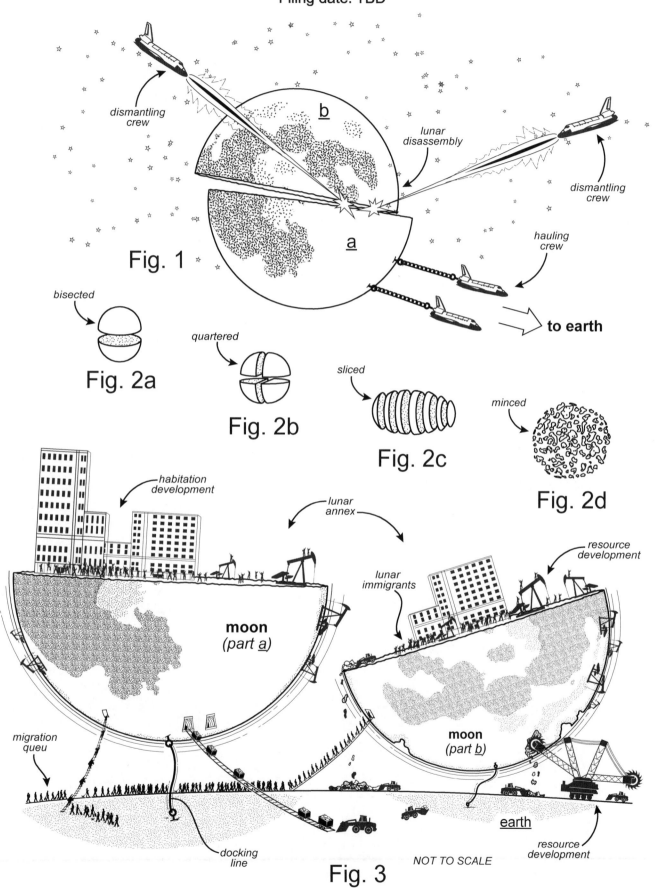

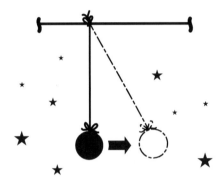

I foresee a day when we can find the perfect place for ourselves in the solar system, free from the annoying temperature swings that can make our planet quite unbearable;

Inventor: Thomas D. W. von Giesler
Title: *An advanced method for planetary relocation.*
Filing date: TBD

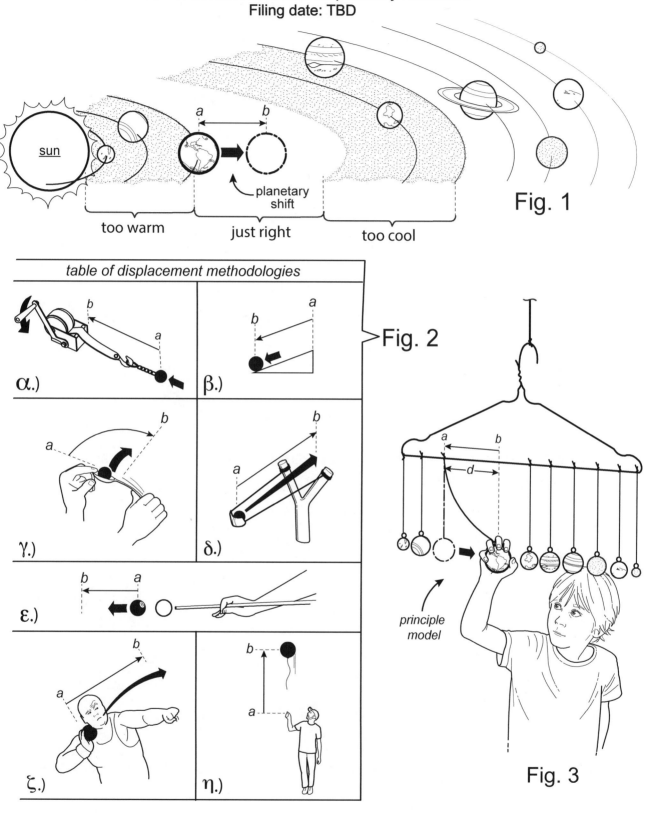

sun

a ← → *b*

planetary shift

too warm

just right

too cool

Fig. 1

table of displacement methodologies

α.)

β.)

γ.)

δ.)

ε.)

ζ.)

η.)

Fig. 2

principle model

Fig. 3

displacement formula:

Fig. 4

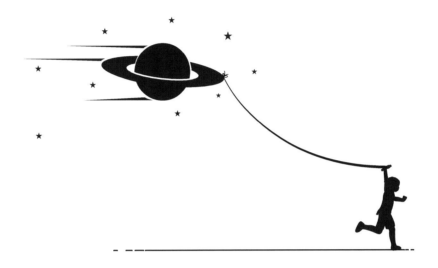

and a day when we assist our neighbors in doing the same.

Inventor: Thomas D. W. von Giesler
Title: *A more advanced method for planet relocation.*
Filing date: TBD

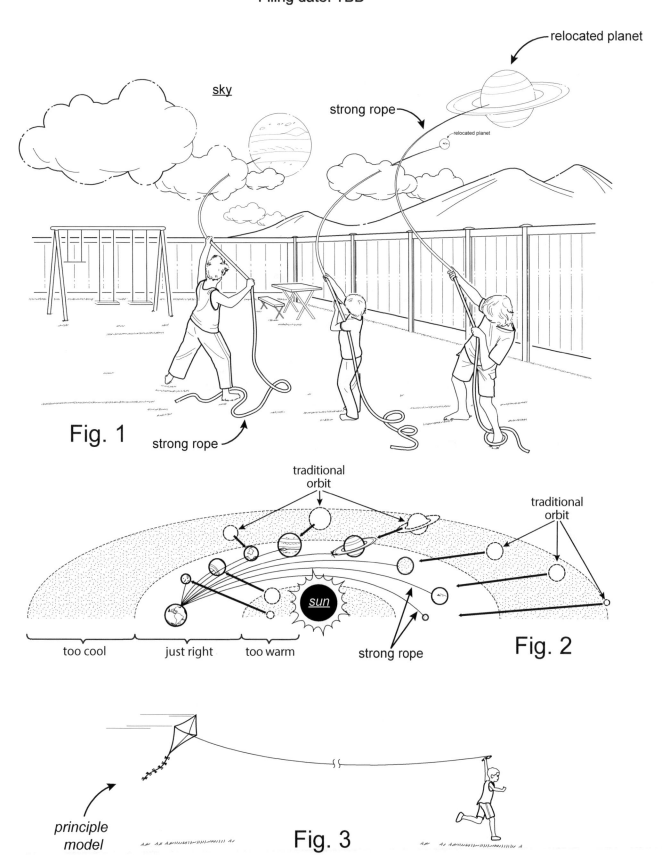

relocated planet

sky

strong rope

relocated planet

Fig. 1

strong rope

traditional orbit

traditional orbit

sun

too cool

just right

too warm

strong rope

Fig. 2

principle model

Fig. 3

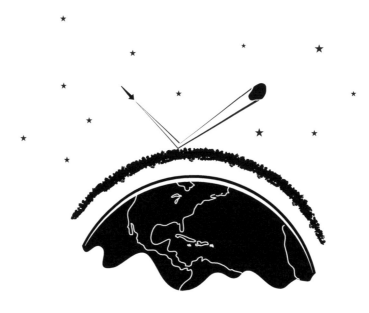

Yes, the real future of this *unventional* movement will require all of us to think globally...

Inventor: Thomas D. W. von Giesler
Title: *An advanced method for creating global security and planetary shade
by infusing orbitable regions with rubbish, refuse, and scrap materials.*
Filing date: TBD

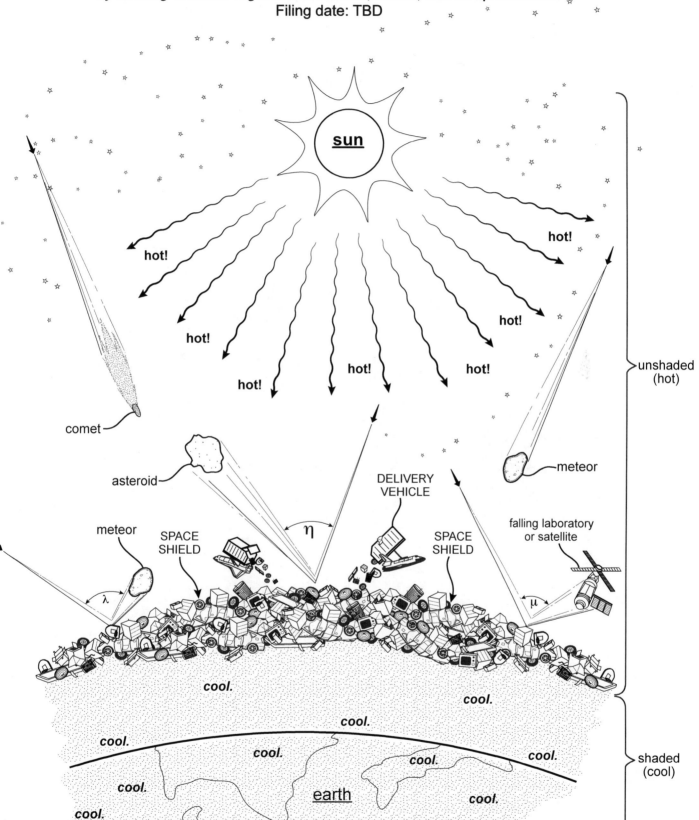

...and act galactically.

Inventor: Thomas D. W. von Giesler
Title: *A very advanced method for poly-planetary, intergalactic migration.*
Filing date: TBD

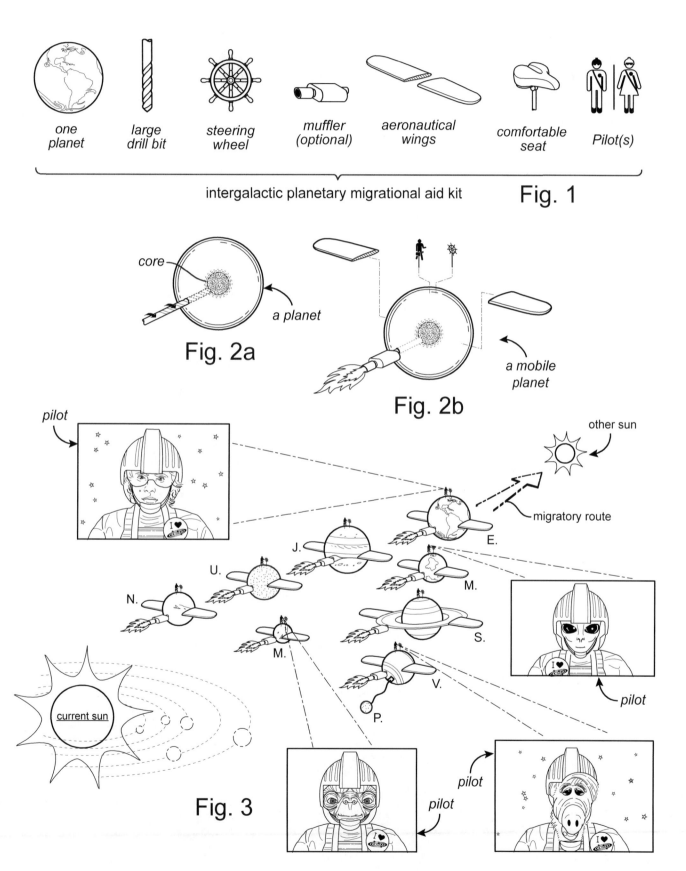

one planet

large drill bit

steering wheel

muffler (optional)

aeronautical wings

comfortable seat

Pilot(s)

intergalactic planetary migrational aid kit

Fig. 1

core

a planet

Fig. 2a

a mobile planet

Fig. 2b

pilot

other sun

migratory route

E.

J.

U.

N.

M.

M.

S.

V.

P.

current sun

pilot

pilot

pilot

pilot

Fig. 3

Made in the USA
Middletown, DE
03 December 2015